BERTRAND RUSSELL'S

THE

ONQUEST OF

HAPPINESS

BERTRAND RUSSELL'S

THE
CONQUEST OF
HAPPINESS

A MODERN-DAY INTERPRETATION
OF A SELF-HELP CLASSIC
BY TIM PHILLIPS

First published in 2010 by
Infinite Ideas Limited
36 St Giles
Oxford, OX1 3LD
United Kingdom
www.infideas.com

A CIP catalogue record for this book is available from the British Library

ISBN 978-1-906821-27-2

Designed and typeset by Cylinder
Printed in Great Britain

BRILLIANT IDEAS

 INTRODUCTION

Bertrand Russell spans two eras. The work he left us shows that he was part of the secular industrial age; often the way he describes it sounds as though he'd travelled from the Victorian age in which he was born (into an aristocratic family) and suddenly been shot forward in a Jules Verne time machine. In *The Conquest of Happiness* he combines a love of skyscrapers and what he called the 'machine age' with complaints about his maid-servants and motor-bicycles. He writes with relish about what the world could become, and with excitement about the possibilities for all of us, but also with the desire that we don't forget the legacy that the great philosophers and novelists have left.

Russell, who eventually won the Nobel Prize for Literature, wrote two kinds of book. His philosophy and mathematics were profound, challenging and accessible only to an educated elite. His popular books, of which *The Conquest of Happiness* is one, were entirely different: easy to read, jokey and open-hearted.

When he's writing about happiness, you get the sense that Russell genuinely cares that we should be happy, and also the sense that he was profoundly, deeply happy himself. This isn't happiness in the giggly, ephemeral sense, but a sense of pleasure in what we experience and a feeling that we are at peace with the world and not easily disappointed with it.

Russell's liberal world view was ahead of its time – he was an atheist, advocate of tolerance for homosexuals, sometime pacifist, anti-nuclear campaigner and a restrained hedonist. He questions ideas, beliefs and ways of thinking that were (and mostly still are) the conventional wisdom, and has the logician's genius of coming up with an answer that appears completely straightforward and obvious – until you try to explain it to someone the next day, and have to go back to look it up again.

Any fool can make complicated things appear complicated. Russell's talent is to make the apparently insoluble problems of 'how can I be happy?' seem manageable by any of us. He writes, he admits, for the majority of people who have health, food and shelter to satisfy their basic needs and who are sometimes happy, but not often enough: a situation many of us know very well.

Russell took his own medicine. His professional life wasn't short of hard choices or disappointment. The difference is that Russell used his remarkable intellect to find ways to avoid despair in that disappointment. Based on his experience, Russell encourages us to take responsibility and not to rely on others, partly out of necessity: when he wrote this book the idea of an antidepressant pill was as likely as someone walking on the moon and the idea that people could 'suffer from stress' was thirty years into the future. For all but a few people, unhappiness wasn't a medical condition. He treats it as a challenge to be overcome. In Russell's world, you help yourself, because you're the best person for the job.

There are many 'self-help' books available that try to make us happier by encouraging us to obsess about ourselves or manipulate others, or both. Russell does neither. From the man who thought for a living for most of his life – and he was ninety-seven when he died – this isn't a book about thinking too much, except where the thinking is useful. So even if it doesn't make you happier, it's likely to save you a lot of time.

1 ALL THE SMALL THINGS

Animal happiness can be a model for our own: clever people don't have a more profound happiness than the rest of us.

Russell begins the book with a Walt Whitman poem about why he likes animals, a preference which we must assume Russell shared. 'They do not sweat and whine about their condition,' the poem says, 'they do not lie awake in the dark and weep for their sins.'

This is, basically, what he's about to propose that we do.

DEFINING IDEA...

I wish I could turn and live with animals, they are so placid and self-contained.

~ WALT WHITMAN

Of course, we don't really know what animals are thinking. I've got a pet turtle, and I'm convinced he likes to watch rugby on TV with me. It doesn't follow from this that watching rugby on TV is a good way to spend time, or that living things who watch TV on a Saturday afternoon instead of, say, walking round Ikea looking for an occasional table, are sensible. I happen to believe this; my wife is not swayed by the Argument From Turtle Preference.

Like Whitman's animals, we don't need to be forever whining and worrying to resolve our problems. Nor, the poem points out, would we be better people if we had the intellect and the will to do so.

But pigs lie around in their own shit and then get made into sausages and neither, we assume, is a reason for celebration for the pig. On the other hand, if you like your own shit, don't cause anyone any harm, and live a fulfilled life before getting slaughtered and ground up into little bits, and accept that whether you die in the slaughterhouse or in a hotel room with a gram of cocaine and five strippers you're still going to die sometime, it's perfectly possible to be intelligently happy in Russell's sense of the word.

Think about it this way. You could spend the next ten minutes thinking 'Why are we here? What are we for? Where are we going? What is the meaning of everything? What happens after death? What's the point?' and I'll lay generous odds that you won't find the answer, be happier, or more fulfilled at the end of that ten minutes.

On the other hand, you could think 'I'm pretty hungry. What's for dinner? I'd really enjoy some Indian food. Maybe I'll text Jim, if he's free we can meet up, I'd like to find out about his trip to Budapest.' There's a fair chance that the result of this will be friendship, a good meal and increased knowledge of central Europe. Is the pleasure we get from these in some way counterfeit, or lacking in depth? On the contrary: delighting in the world around us, and truly living in it to the best of our ability, says Russell, is the root of the most profound happiness we can experience.

HERE'S AN IDEA FOR YOU...

Hedonism isn't about overindulgence, it's about taking pleasure in the world around you. Got friends who are just back from Budapest, or any friends you haven't seen for too long? Call them now. Meet them. The next chapter will still be here when you get back.

2 YOUR HAPPINESS IS YOUR BUSINESS

Thinking for yourself isn't always easy: in many cases it can be uncomfortable to confront our needs, desires, prejudices and urges. But for Russell, this is the route to happiness.

Achieving happiness is the great struggle of our lives. Yet we often treat it as a by-product of the other things we do such as work, marriage, family, shopping. It's not: it's the essence of what we strive to be.

DEFINING IDEA...

If you don't change your beliefs, your life will be like this forever. Is that good news?
– WILLIAM SOMERSET MAUGHAM

A path to knowledge, Bertrand Russell style: we experience things, we break them down into their simplest form, we form opinions, we build up those opinions into a view of ourselves and our place in the world. If you're thinking 'everybody does that', you're right and wrong. We all learn from our experiences, but rarely by reflecting on those experiences.

Today we are fed our opinions in indigestible chunks by politicians, the media and would-be demagogues. It's the frustration and the delight of reading Russell that he often tells us to work it out for ourselves. He offers what he considers to be basic truths: that we can't rely on a god to sort things out for us (and certainly not in a way that will promote our personal happiness), that many of the principles by which we are raised are not designed to make us happy, and that we all have the capability to be happy through taking action, rather than waiting for happiness to be thrust upon us.

Russell's book is full of his challenges to the status quo: how we work, how we respond to competition, how we learn and think about sex – all these are, he says, fundamentally wrong if we want to make ourselves happier.

But it's the process of thinking yourself happy that will seem most alien to us. We're accustomed to shopping ourselves happy, medicating ourselves happy or drinking ourselves happy; even if they don't work, we're definitely giving all three our best shot.

To follow his advice, we need to accept two things. The first is that money and success are not the same thing. It's easy for a home-schooled heir to an earldom who was acclaimed as the greatest philosopher of the twentieth century to say that, but Russell never departed from this principle, and was not rich. The second is that it's possible to be wrong, and when you are wrong, it's your responsibility to change the way you think, the way you act, so as to maximise the happiness of yourself and the people around you. Russell delighted not in finding all the answers, but in asking the hardest questions.

Happiness, being the most valuable attribute of our lives, isn't presented as easy, or as a right. He shows us how to earn it, and to get anything out of this book you have to be prepared to change everything and anything about yourself. Are you ready?

HERE'S AN IDEA FOR YOU...

Russell's favourite Bible verse, 'thou shalt not follow a multitude to do evil', expressed his desire to make his own mind up. Is there something you do, just because the people around you do it, that makes you unhappy? Now's the time to cut it out.

3 DUMBING UP

When Russell left his life in an ivory tower behind, he discovered that he had some excellent advice for the rest of us, but he avoids a quick fix – as should we.

DEFINING IDEA...

Make everything as simple as possible, but not simpler.
– ALBERT EINSTEIN.

Until his mid-forties, Russell believed that philosophy was an elitist discipline. In his hands, it usually was. He had little interest in taking the results of his thought into the wider world and using it for practical purposes. He discovered that in the 1920s and 1930s people were just as interested in how to better their lives, and in what the great thinkers of the day thought were good ways to do this, as they are today.

This happy accident served Russell well; he could turn out books on education, religion and marriage, as well as regular newspaper columns, at the drop of a hat. By the time he won the Nobel Prize, he had a pretty dusty hat.

Was this 'dumbing down'? No. It was popularising. The differences are subtle but important. The first is that Russell was self-aware. 'No profound philosophy will be found in the following pages,' he warns us. 'I venture to hope that some among the multitude of men and women who suffer unhappiness without enjoying it, may find this situation diagnosed and a method of escape suggested.'

On the other hand, he doesn't boil down his logic into useless soundbytes. His book doesn't seek to give us the happiness we require at a price we desire.

It doesn't wash blue moods whiter. It doesn't give us five smiles a day or ten tips for fun, or claim to be a foolproof guide.

Today football managers and CEOs have to have a 'philosophy' as part of the job. You probably have a friend who claims to have a 'philosophy of life', which is usually along the lines of 'never apologise'. This isn't so much a philosophy as a route to obnoxiousness.

When Russell engages with the 'multitude of men and women' he doesn't fall into the trap of promising success or attaching easy labels to difficult concepts, and he doesn't guarantee easy results. He doesn't reassure us that achieving happiness is easy: the book promises a 'conquest', suggesting an arduous battle that it's easy to lose. In short, he doesn't dumb down what, for many of us, is the hardest and most confusing struggle of our lives: the struggle to be happy.

Instead he offers a far richer future for us. His method? Thinking clearly and reaching a conclusion from first principles. He shows us the value of logic and the therapeutic value of taking control of our own thoughts and ignoring easy solutions.

Today, happiness is an industry. Russell makes us see the potential in our lives by doing what few of today's self-help books or hectoring magazine articles or oversimplified TV programmes do: he treats us like adults, and he expects that we should do the same for ourselves.

HERE'S AN IDEA FOR YOU...

If you're a self-help junkie, take another look at the books, CD-Roms, magazines and Internet guides that you have invested time and money in over the years. If they aren't helping, throw them away. At the very least, you'll get some more shelf space.

4 BUYING HAPPINESS

Material things cannot, on their own, deliver happiness. History tells us so.

The first half of Russell's (and our) book is about the causes of unhappiness, of which there are many in Russell's view. There's better news later. 'If you are happy, ask yourself how many of your friends are,' he says, adding that 'unhappiness meets you everywhere'.

There's nothing more tiresome than being at a social occasion where everyone is so determined to be happy that it's impossible for anyone to enjoy themselves. New Year is the best example, but family birthdays (especially your own), stag and hen nights, visits to relatives, special events featuring the offspring of friends and luxury holidays can all produce a similar effect.

We spend a lot of effort and a considerable amount of money in the pursuit of happiness, or rather in the denial of unhappiness. Often, as Russell points out, we are prepared to deny what we know about ourselves or our friends in this hysterical hunt: we repeat events that don't make us happy in the hope that something will change.

So the first thing we have to accept is that you – well, all of us – are often not happy. Or, at least, could be happier – and that this is not shameful or weird. Research that Russell didn't have shows that our external circumstances have, for most of us, little to do with our feelings of happiness. The Pew Research

Center in the US has been asking people how happy they have been feeling for almost forty years, through recessions and booms, advances in healthcare and technology. The numbers stay the same: about half of Americans are fairly happy. About 30% are very happy. The rest are unhappy.

There will always be some in the bottom group whose unhappiness, we could assume, would take more than a book to alter. If you are homeless, or experience chronic pain, or are unjustly imprisoned, or have some form of mental illness, unhappiness is pretty much unavoidable.

For the rest of us, our circumstances are much improved compared to forty years ago. The Pew statistic shows that cars, exotic holidays, the Internet, satellite TV and refillable air fresheners don't deliver happiness.

We can, however, resolve to do what Russell wants, and that is to stop trying to find happiness solely in the double-edged pleasures of the outside world. Most of us can change, even if we feel sometimes that we can't. We can take control, and we can do more of what makes us happy, and less of what makes us unhappy.

Russell was aware of the people in 1930 who went out at New Year 'determined to be happy'. Unless we recognise that material things don't deliver happiness, every day will be like New Year's Eve.

HERE'S AN IDEA FOR YOU...

Do you have an event, a commitment (or even some friends) that you endure regularly, forcing a smile? Admit to yourself that you hate it, you always hated it and you always will. It might not be easy to get out of it, but you're not going to be happy until you try.

5 THE ME GENERATION

Russell believed that our unhappiness begins with our preoccupation with ourselves and our shortcomings. Only involvement with other people and things can solve the problem.

Despite being born into a wealthy and noble family, and being identified at an early age as a prodigiously clever young viscount, Russell reveals he was a glum kid – even at the age of five.

'I was not born happy,' he says. 'In adolescence I hated life and was continually on the verge of suicide, from which, however, I was restrained by the desire to know more mathematics.'

DEFINING IDEA...

I, not events, have the power to make me happy or unhappy today.
~ GROUCHO MARX

A suicidal teenager who keeps himself alive with the promise of extra maths. That's about as bad as it gets. Russell did, though, climb out of that hole thanks to, as he tells us 'a diminishing preoccupation with myself'. He got absorbed in his studies – it helps that he was one of the most exceptional minds of the twentieth century, so there was a lot to do – and gradually cured himself of his melancholy.

What can we learn from this, except the insight that what might extinguish suicidal feelings in Bertrand Russell often creates suicidal feelings in the rest of us? That we can be happier if we immerse ourselves in the struggles and challenges that bring us most satisfaction. Russell believes that this is simply because we are then given time off from the puritan focus on our own 'follies and shortcomings' which we are conditioned to obsess about.

There are two good examples of our inward-looking obsession. The first, Russell points out, is that we love a good melancholy booze-up, especially in Northern Europe. While Russell understood the lure of getting pissed when you're pissed off, he also understood the danger of obliterating your unhappiness for a few hours rather than doing anything with it. 'Drunkenness is temporary suicide,' he said.

Here's a more modern example of the effect. In 2006 *Top Sante* magazine questioned 2000 women over 40 about what they thought of their bodies. The average score was 3.5 out of 10. Almost six out of ten women admitted that they would eat in a disordered way to try to lose weight, including taking laxatives. The average respondent wanted to lose two stone in weight, and admitted to feelings of envy when seeing women whose bodies they admired.

Our obsession with unattainable body image – even when having that body would create health problems – is encouraged by magazines that purport to entertain and educate us. We're our own favourite subject, even though ultimately this appears to give us little satisfaction.

We can't all use a genius for mathematics to cure ourselves of morbid self-obsession, but we owe it to ourselves to do more than just wish we were happier. For a man whose life was dedicated to thought, Russell's advice if you want to be happy is to do something.

HERE'S AN IDEA FOR YOU...

As the young Russell did, make the choice. Do you choose to be happy or unhappy? If you choose happiness, he further asks, will trying to be happy do any harm? If the answer is no, then start trying.

6 IT WON'T MAKE ANY DIFFERENCE

Russell thinks the habit of attributing some sort of intellectual credibility to people who see the world as hopeless as silly: when there's no guarantee of a happy ending, it is still reasonable to hope.

What Russell calls 'Byronic unhappiness' – the argument that all human life is characterised by misery, and always will be, and so the only appropriate response is to be miserable – isn't, in his view, attributable to the 'nature of the universe'.

DEFINING IDEA...

'Good morning, Pooh Bear,' said Eeyore gloomily. 'If it is a good morning,' he said. 'Which I doubt.'
~ A. A. MILNE, WINNIE THE POOH

Actually, it's a bit rough on Lord Byron, whose zest and energy Russell would have respected.

It's natural to be unhappy as a response to the shocking cruelty of individual events: wars, poverty, natural disasters, crimes against family and friends, unfairness. If, when you heard about these things, you simply shrugged and said 'that's life', you wouldn't be so much happy as disconnected – especially if the misfortunes happened to you.

So unhappiness at times is natural. But there is not, Russell says, a 'superior rationality' in being unhappy. His counter-argument takes in natural selection, soap operas and skyscrapers.

First, we are, he says, adapted for struggle, and so we take greater pleasure in the things that we strive for than the things that are given to us. This is a biological imperative. 'The man who acquires easily things for which he feels only a moderate desire concludes that the attainment of his desires does not bring happiness,' he writes. So disappointment, unhappiness and frustration are components of a happy life. They make us strive for more; they don't tell us that striving is hopeless.

This isn't to say that a struggle will bring satisfaction. Russell also points out that a life is not a scripted melodrama 'in which the hero and heroine go through incredible misfortunes for which they are compensated by a happy ending'. So hoping for an end result isn't a way to happiness.

What can we do? Russell, despite being fifty-eight years old in 1930 when this book was published, recommends being excited by possibility. He fully engaged with the world he saw: skyscrapers, broadcasting and aeroplanes showed that change could be good, and make us happier. To that we could add antibiotics, good television, rock and roll, football. New events can change us for ever by showing us the possibility of a happy life. As he points out, we go on holiday and come back to the same place but that doesn't mean the holiday didn't have any value.

The idea of a world in which we are doomed to Byronic unhappiness is a one-sided argument which can be alluring. Eventually, though, it's not deep or profound to take this attitude. Far better to accept the world as it is, with no guarantees, and from that to relish its pleasures.

HERE'S AN IDEA FOR YOU...

If you are experiencing prolonged unhappiness in a job 'that will look good on your CV', or not changing your situation because 'it won't make any difference', you are a slave to Byronic unhappiness. Hope for happiness, and make changes now to achieve it.

7 THE FUTURE ISN'T WHAT IT USED TO BE

Was everything better in the past? Not often.

In a cave in the south of France, some of the earliest paintings on the rock show hunts for buffalo, using only spears. The inscription at the bottom, roughly translated, says 'I'm sure these spears used to be sharper'.

DEFINING IDEA...

The scientist is not a person who gives the right answers, he's one who asks the right questions.
– CLAUDE LÉVI-STRAUSS

All right, that's made up. But Russell points out that in the thirteenth century Roger Bacon, one of the first great Western philosophers and deep thinkers, wrote that 'More sins reign in these days of ours than in any past age.' In the 800 years that has passed since then, many other writers less perceptive and intelligent than Bacon have responded to progress in a similar way. You only have to pick up the *Daily Mail* to discover that we're about to descend into a hell of our own making caused by asylum seekers, social workers, young people – anyone but us.

At some points, for some people, this has been true. You can't say, with hindsight, that the First World War was a change for the better compared to life in Edwardian Britain. But for the majority of us, most of the time, each generation has been able to do more, for longer, with more freedom, than the last. For this, especially in the last 200 years, we have science to thank.

And yet we are frightened, confused and intimidated by progress, by the advance of technology. Stem-cell research, nuclear power, cloning and social networking give most of us a sense of unease that may occasionally be justified.

Russell says that if we think it's the job of scientific progress simply to answer questions, then we're not going to be happy. It cannot 'make promises,' he says, or 'satisfy our infantile desire for safety and protection'.

Safety and protection are perfectly reasonable desires, but if we want them without getting involved with their source, understanding it or choosing it, then we are literally acting like children. We have to first understand that science doesn't answer every question, but only proposes ideas and frameworks with which to find those answers – and also that it is a tool that can have bad outcomes (the atomic bomb) as well as good (non-iron shirts).

It might seem rather cool to say that you don't understand science, as if you are somehow made more perceptive by understanding only a small part of what goes on around you. If you don't understand, you are condemned to be passive – pining for an age of innocence which, if you'd lived in it, would have seen you saying things like 'I don't understand these wheel things, and I'm not sure I didn't prefer it when everything stayed where you put it.' Refusing to accept the present cannot deliver happiness.

HERE'S AN IDEA FOR YOU...

Does something about the modern world intimidate you secretly? Take a week, read everything about it. Stop worrying and start understanding. Make an opinion from fact, not fear.

8 TOUGH LOVE

Russell was brought up by his grandparents in a loveless Victorian style. He never forgot it. His life was a search for the adventure of love, and he says that yours should be too.

'The kind of love I believe in is not the kind the Victorians admired,' Russell says. 'It is adventurous and open-eyed.'

A fifty-eight-year-old, posh, white-haired philosopher with a prison record and a couple of divorces behind him, Russell might have been a hard man to love by conventional standards. But people, having the feelings that inspire them to cooperate, he reasoned, should not be solitary if it can be avoided. They should seek out company and inspiration and, dare we say it, fun.

The romantic view of love, a bloke sitting alone on top of a mountain feeling wistful and sad, isn't his model, nor should it be ours. Love isn't the alternative to worldly things, he says, it's the catalyst for the best of them, especially sex. 'Love is to be valued because it enhances all the best pleasures,' he writes, because it means you can 'break down the hard shell of the ego'.

For Freud, the ego was the part of the unconscious which checked and controlled the impulse to seek pleasure of the id: 'The ego represents what may be called reason and common sense, in contrast to the id, which contains the passions,' he wrote, seven years before Russell published his book. The ego serves an important function (it makes us civilised) but it also controls those powerful urges and desires which give us pure pleasure.

And so, Russell says, finding love isn't about discovering someone you admire, or someone who buys things for you, or someone who will tell you how wonderful you are. It's about finding someone to help you experience pleasure, and for whom you can do the same.

There's an episode of the cult comedy *Seinfeld* where Jerry Seinfeld meets Jeannie Steinman, a girlfriend whom he hits it off with immediately, because she's just like him. She likes cereal and Superman just like him, she speaks the same way, she makes the same jokes. He can't believe his luck. They get engaged. At the beginning of the next episode, Jerry's friend asks him how the engagement is going:

Jerry: There's really not that much to tell.

[flashback as Jerry narrates.] About a month ago, we were here having lunch, when all of a sudden we both just blurted out...

Jerry and Jeannie: (simultaneously) I hate you!

Often, Russell says, we are too preoccupied with ourselves to find lasting love. We seek a match, not the possibility of happiness through shared experience. Yet love, though uncommon, changes us: 'In its highest form it reveals values which must otherwise remain unknown,' he states. So look for love, but think about the adventures of the future, not the present.

HERE'S AN IDEA FOR YOU...

Remember when you met your significant other and you were happy to do all sorts of things you wouldn't normally do, in and out of the bedroom? Now is the time to rekindle one of those adventures. If Russell can, you can too.

9 NOT GREAT MEN

Just because you're not exceptional doesn't mean you don't have a right to be happy.

DEFINING IDEA...

God must love the common man, he made so many of them.

– ABRAHAM LINCOLN

The years between the wars saw, for the first time, the idea generally expressed that everyone had the right to be happy, and that everyone deserved that right. Perhaps it was the Russian revolution and the widespread admiration for communism among the intellectual classes (Russell got caught up in this, of which more later). Maybe it was the simple fact that more 'ordinary' people could express themselves and be seen and heard, from D. H. Lawrence's muscular heroes to the frustration of T.S. Eliot's middle-aged Prufrock. For the first time we see the idea commonly held that poor people, uneducated or powerless people desired and deserved happiness.

It's not so surprising for us to hear this. But we are still programmed to believe from an early age that only great people (however we measure greatness) have a tragic dimension to their unhappiness, while the rest of us are just a bit sad.

Russell praises *Ghosts*, a play written fifty years earlier by Henrik Ibsen, in comparison to *King Lear*. In it, a widow who conforms to Victorian and religious morality in the face of her husband's infidelity is still ruined by it, as are her son and his lover. If you've ever seen it performed, it's not a lot of laughs – as plays about syphilis generally aren't – but it is properly tragic in that she is basically good and her flaw brings about her downfall, and those of the people closest to her. But why should we care about the story of an ordinary woman?

Why not? asks Russell. 'We no longer regard certain individuals as the great ones of the earth, who have a right to tragic passion, while all the rest must merely drudge and toil,' he says. High tragedy, he adds, is communal, something that arises from the way in which we live, not something that happens to an individual.

It seems obvious now, and the old idea that happiness is not 'for the likes of us' seems quaint. But it's still programmed into our unconscious minds by daily news coverage. It's implicit that a man who loses a few million but still has a few million left in the bank is somehow much harder done by than those of us who will never have that kind of money, or his house, or his experiences, or his opportunities. When a famous person gets cancer it's sad, but no sadder for the planet than if your neighbour had the same diagnosis. In a perfect world we'd give all the news, good and bad, about everyone, the same emphasis. On the other hand it wouldn't be a perfect world: we'd have to have TV channels showing nothing but news twenty-four hours a day. Imagine how tedious that would be.

The rich, the famous and the privileged have bad times – but no worse than ours.

HERE'S AN IDEA FOR YOU...

Go cold turkey on celebrity gossip for at least a week. Preferably for thirty or forty years. Look closer to home for inspiration, for people who need help and support: your neighbours, your friends, your colleagues at work.

10 SPEAK YOUR BRAINS

Everybody's got a book in them – if we include ignorant, boring or dull books. The trick to expressing yourself, Russell says, isn't the words; it's knowing what you're talking about.

DEFINING IDEA...

Can a man who's warm understand one who's freezing?
– ALEXANDER SOLZHENITSYN

And so we get to an end of our wide-ranging exploration of Byronic unhappiness – the silly idea that in some way it is profound or noble to be unhappy, that happy people are simple, and that the greatest emotions are reserved for great thinkers. These ideas, Russell says, come from our tendency to get trapped inside ourselves, to ignore the evidence of the outside world that things can be better, that new and unexpected events can be good.

Or that meeting people and trying new ideas is superior to sitting at home and worrying about questions to which there are no answers.

Russell wasn't a blogger, what with there being no blogs and no Internet on which to post them, but he was a popular writer. His output demonstrates that he wasn't short of material; there's no evidence of writer's block. The words tumbled out of him because of his experiences. For example, when he talks about not worrying whether people approve of your views, he had been sacked and imprisoned for his published opinions.

He has this advice to any of you who want to write, but don't know how to get started: 'Give up trying to write, and instead try not to write. Go out into the world: become a pirate, a King in Borneo, a labourer in Soviet Russia.' Only then, he reasons, will you have something to write about.

Eighty years on, we shouldn't be taking this too literally. Even at the time, the only one of his suggested experiences which produced great literature was the third one – and great though *The Gulag Archipelago* is as literature, it was arduous for Alexander Solzhenitsyn to do the research. What matters is Russell's advice to experience the world before you condemn it. Don't write about the contents of your own head.

So it is with the blogosphere, much of which confirms that often the desire to write outstrips the desire to know. As a way to pass time it's fine, but ultimately, Russell says, writing without direct experience of what we write is a waste of time and cannot bring us happiness, because it still traps us inside ourselves, looking out at a world we don't properly understand.

If the would-be writer were to become a pirate (not recommended) or King of Borneo (not easily done without redrawing some national borders), Russell says, 'His writing will not seem to him futile.' But, he points out, what might also happen is that he finds something else to do.

Here's a modern equivalent. In Russell's time the idea that someone should go into politics direct from university would have been laughable, and yet today we have a professional political class who do exactly that. Should members of parliament have second jobs? There are strong arguments against it, but the most powerful argument in its favour is that experience gives us satisfaction when we express ourselves, and makes us more useful human beings.

HERE'S AN IDEA FOR YOU...

Don't give money to charity, give your time. Volunteering gives something just as valuable as cash, and gives something back to you that you can't find elsewhere.

11 A WORLD OF SNARK

Our inability to escape competitiveness is creating a world in which every opinion has to be undermined: the quality which the critic David Denby refers to as 'snark'.

And so to competition. 'The emphasis on competition in modern life is connected with a general decay in civilised standards,' Russell writes, 'men and women appear incapable of enjoying the more intellectual pleasures.'

DEFINING IDEA...

It's all jeer and josh, a form that...
beggars the soul of humour.
– DAVID DENBY

He lamented the decay of the art of conversation and that we no longer seem to relish good literature or the world around us. 'Some American students took me walking in the spring through a wood on the borders of their campus,' he recalls, 'it was filled with exquisite wild flowers, but not one of my guides knew the name even of one of them. What use would such knowledge be? It could not add to anybody's income.'

The trouble, he says, has little to do with an individual's lack of curiosity about flowers, or dedication to conversation, or indifference to long books full of difficult words. 'The trouble arises from the generally received philosophy of life, according to which life is a contest, a competition, in which respect is to be accorded to the victor.'

In his book of the same name, Denby laments our modern tendency to use 'snark' – a contraction of 'snide' and 'remark'. He's not, as the great conversationalists of eighteenth-century France were not, against rudeness and satire when it's required; he thinks rudeness has its place. What he objects to is the writer, conversationalist and blog commentator who basically says that everything is rubbish. Great satire, he says, implies a better world. Great criticism attempts to reform what is criticised, even if this is hopeless. Snark merely attempts to destroy.

Common-or-garden snark is easy to spot. When we roll our eyes at a colleague's success for no better reason than we all collectively resent it, when we read a blog argument followed by a stream of posts attacking the person and not the argument, and when we listen to politicians attacking each other as a means of avoiding the necessity of telling us what they would do instead, we're victims of snark.

A common element of snark, in Denby's description of it, is that the snarker primarily wants to undermine, and perhaps to replace, the snarkee. Ultimately, what separates it from serious, justified criticism – which can be accepted or argued against, and potentially offers growth for everyone involved, no matter how tough it is at the time – is that snark is a sublimated form of competition. It's a way to undermine your competitor when you have only negative tactics with which to do it. The Internet, social networking, open-plan offices and text messaging have greatly expanded the possibility of amateur snark, and many of us are very good at it. Just remember: snarking says more about the snark than it does about you.

HERE'S AN IDEA FOR YOU...

Snarkers have no defence against confidence. When someone rudely dismisses your new job by making fun of the pathetic salary, remind yourself that the money wasn't why you took it. When someone ridicules the way you dress, remember that they probably envy your self-confidence.

12 WORK–LIFE MADNESS

Competition, Russell says, is the root of much of our unhappiness, as we ruin our lives by striving for trivial outcomes which give us no pleasure. Sorry if that sounds like your job.

The struggle of the office worker, Russell concludes (using the sort of language that perhaps only someone who has never worked in an office could use) is 'to give dignity to something essentially trivial'.

He presents a picture of the average office worker in 1930 which isn't so different from today – only in 1930 you didn't have to take your BlackBerry on holiday with you. He objects to the false importance that the career ladder is given. It's the struggle for success, to be better than your neighbours.

Russell's office worker gets up before dawn to hurry to the office, gets home late at night 'just in time to dress for dinner' – it is 1930, after all – which he pretends to enjoy. 'Year by year he grows more lonely' as he doesn't know his wife or his children, and when he's on holiday he's thinking about work.

Recognise that? Not the bit about dressing for dinner, obviously. The rest of it.

We hear a lot about work–life balance, often from companies which sell you gadgets which claim to be designed to enhance this. At least that's their story.

Often these gadgets are designed to spoil your holiday by allowing your boss to send you emails at the beach.

It's disconcerting, though not uncommon, to visit a public toilet and hear someone answering a call inside one of the cubicles. Installing software to do tasks faster doesn't mean you finish earlier, it means you are given more tasks.

The only real work–life balance comes from inside your own head. A mobile computer can't bring you happiness, but the ability to switch off your mind (and your phone) can.

What might you sacrifice? Money, probably, and status in the eyes of those who value money above happiness. 'The businessman's religion and glory demand that he should make much money; therefore... he suffers the torment gladly,' Russell writes. Money can make us happy to a point, but the pursuit of money and power for its own sake, rather than as part of a wider plan to achieve happiness for you and your family, can bring just as much unhappiness to you and to those around you.

We love to talk about entrepreneurs, hyper growth, risk takers and billionaires, but research shows that many small businesses don't want to grow – the people in them just want a better life, to see more of their kids, or have a little more security. Why do we consider that shameful?

HERE'S AN IDEA FOR YOU...

You can't switch off until you switch off. Schedule time during which you promise yourself and your family that you won't work, talk about work or worry about work. Switch off the phone, shut the laptop. They need it as much as you do.

13 LITERATURE'S RETURN ON INVESTMENT

Do we admire people who are good at what they do, or who have become rich through what they do?

'Money made is the accepted measure of brains,' laments Russell in his chapter on competition, admonishing us all for judging every achievement on how much money can be made from it.

DEFINING IDEA...

All that non-fiction can do is answer questions. It's fiction's business to ask them.

~ RICHARD HUGHES

A few years ago I was at a conference dinner where some awards were to be given. At our table sat an eminent man in his industry, who was to be honoured in the final award of the evening, the one that recognised a lifetime of contribution to the industry concerned. He was an innovator, a broad and accomplished thinker in his field.

During the evening we talked about his career. Each time we asked about a job, or a project, he replied with how much money it had made for his employer. When we asked what he achieved, he told us about his cars and houses. When the table got tired of this and started to discuss novels that we liked, he was silent.

'What's your favourite novel?' asked the woman sitting on his right.

'My father taught me not to read novels,' he said, 'There's no return on investment.'

It's true: in financial terms, there's no return on investment for reading a book, even this one. If, instead of working eighteen hours a day through his thirties and forties, that man had left work on time and gone to the park with a book, he'd certainly have had less money in the bank. He wouldn't have been given a lifetime achievement award by a group of people, many of whom shared his suspicion of literature. On the other hand, he would have been able to take part in a fulfilling conversation with five other people, which might have contributed more to his lasting happiness.

This isn't an argument for forcing children to read books. Russell is simply pointing out that the standard that equates success with money will make more people unhappy than it makes happy, and leads to a way of living your life which values transactions – the goal – over experience.

That eminent man might have had a narrow education, but at least he was honest. We are so goal-oriented that many of us don't just not read books but, as Russell points out, we pretend that we have. A survey by Populus in 2008 shows that one third of women and half of men have lied about reading a book to impress other people. Newspapers print jokey book summaries so you can bluff. One in five adults admitted to reading a book before going on a date so they could sound impressive.

Reading books might not make you happy, but not reading and pretending you do – that's far more likely to make you unhappy.

HERE'S AN IDEA FOR YOU...

Instead of filling your house with impressive-looking books that you don't read just to impress people, join a library. You get to experience the true value of books by freeing yourself from the need to collect them. And it's free. No matter how little you like the book, that's a pretty good return on investment.

14 HOW TO BE BORED

Boredom and idleness are not the same as unhappiness. In fact, Russell considers them essential to our well-being.

'Wars, persecutions and pogroms have all been part of the flight from boredom,' Russell believes. Indeed, only nine years after *The Conquest of Happiness* was published, one evening Hitler was aimlessly twiddling the dials on his Bakelite radio when he turned to Goering and said 'Will we go to the pub or invade Poland?'

This is bad boredom. But Russell says there is good boredom too.

DEFINING IDEA...

The cure for boredom is curiosity. There is no cure for curiosity.
– ELLEN PARR

So let's deal with the good stuff first. Boredom as the 'contrast between the present and another imagined state' is, Russell says, a necessary idea if you want to become happier and more fulfilled. Bored people will rise up as one, rent that interesting Polish film from the video library, sign up for a pottery class, finally wire up their computers properly so that they work as they were meant to.

We are genetically programmed not to like boredom, Russell says, because our ancestors were hunters. When we settled down to plant things and domesticate animals, life became duller. We were saved from this by the machine age, which 'enormously diminished the sum of boredom in the world'.

This was written by a man who didn't have to wait on the line for a call centre or go through his spam folder, but Russell's overall point is that, compared to the Victorians who brought him into the world and who are now only seen in costume dramas, it's pretty easy to be stimulated. As he says, in those days there was little to do after supper except sit around and look bored.

Russell's insight is that if we don't relish our boredom, we'll never learn to value it. We will continue to do things not because they're valuable, but because we need to do things. The result isn't a satisfying day, but a full one.

An occasionally quiet life is 'a characteristic of great men,' he says: 'their pleasures have not been of the sort that would look exciting to the outward eye'. Because they could happily empty their minds and pause to think, their boredom would give way not to excitement, but to fulfilment. Darwin would spend the morning walking around his garden, following the same path, as he thought through his problems. Newton would, on occasion, be gripped by a thought as he got out of bed, and spend hours, motionless, thinking about it.

Productivity guru David Allen, who has worked with everyone from Google to the US Navy, advises that you spend half an hour a week just thinking about the things you have to do. Don't do anything. Just think. Get it straight in your mind. Learning to do nothing and reflect, he says, makes doing everything else more productive.

HERE'S AN IDEA FOR YOU...

If you habitually work while watching TV, do your email while you're talking on the phone, or send text messages while having dinner, take a week where you do one thing at once, as well as you can do it. Don't be scared that it's not exciting enough.

15 BAD BOREDOM

The danger of boredom is that we think the cure has to be thrill-seeking. We crave events. We are addicted to adrenaline which makes us more excited but, in the long run, not happier.

'All great books contain boring portions,' Russell says, joking that if you gave the Old Testament to a modern publisher he would complain that 'this chapter lacks pep'. These days 'every housemaid expects at least once a week as much excitement as would have lasted a Jane Austen heroine throughout a whole novel'.

Two points to make about this. One: once a week does not seem exactly unreasonable, even for one's housemaid. Two: Jane Austen heroines, though far more real than Katie Price or Madonna to most of us, didn't actually exist.

Russell's point is that all of us, young and old, rich and poor, expect to be entertained constantly.

Everywhere we look we find stimulation. Cars are advertised as 'fun to drive', as if getting us from one place to another were merely a useful by-product of their function. Kid's trainers have flashing lights or little wheels, because shoes lack entertainment value. Only twenty-five years ago television used to finish around midnight and start again at breakfast time. Shops look like nightclubs, nightclubs are shops. Once I went on a cruise for three days, and during the last meal the head waiter announced, 'Ladies and gentlemen, pray silence for the PARADE OF BAKED ALASKA!' At which point, accompanied by the

'March of the Toreadors', waiters processed around the restaurant carrying flaming puddings. We were so addicted to constant stimulation that we would have applauded a pig's bladder on a stick. We nearly started a riot – though I'm sure that five minutes later no one could have told you why.

Too much excitement, Russell points out, is 'like a person with a morbid craving for pepper'. It's not that we shouldn't be excited, unless we have a heart condition, or were seeking work as Russell's housemaid. It's that when we're constantly stimulated, it 'dulls our palate' for other pleasures. So, as he puts it, titillation replaces satisfaction. Cleverness replaces wisdom. 'Jagged surprise' replaces beauty.

A life of titillation, cleverness and surprise doesn't sound too bad if you are living in deepest Lincolnshire, but in reality it's like feeding ourselves emotional sweets when we need a salad. If we're on a metaphorical (or literal) roller coaster, we have no time to attend to our deeper unhappiness, or to make the changes we need to improve our lives when the roller coaster stops.

If we can't break away from the need for instant gratification, we become its slave, eating a packet of biscuits before dinner, losing interest in real partners because we're addicted to porn, unable to sit through a film with character and plot because it doesn't have enough car chases and explosions. Ultimately, we become excited infants – as Russell described it, 'a generation of little men'.

HERE'S AN IDEA FOR YOU...

Meditation isn't about silencing the voices in your head; it's about giving yourself a quiet time to listen to them. You don't need a guru or a CD to do that, but you do need the will to stop looking for excitement for thirty minutes.

16 ARE YOU SITTING FORWARD?

We're so busy acting, we often don't have time to think. The trouble with interaction is that it's simply distraction; at times, it's better to listen to others, or to ourselves.

DEFINING IDEA...

Any activity becomes creative when the doer cares about doing it right or better.

~ JOHN UPDIKE

Text us your opinion of this chapter. Or, alternatively, don't. Just think about it.

Russell complained that children, especially, were being given 'far too many passive amusements' for his taste. As a young man who had amused himself with quadratic equations and the ontological argument for the existence of a god, he was quite used to making his own fun. He existed happily with his own brain for company, and the two of them had a long and happy working life together.

Today we convince ourselves that we don't educate children, or adults, passively. Switch on twenty-four-hour news or talk radio and you'll be lucky if you go twenty-four minutes without being asked to text, phone or email your opinion, often all three. It's impossible for snow to fall without someone on a website or a TV programme asking you to send a picture of it. Buddhist monks would ask that if a tree fell in the forest and nobody heard it, would it make a sound? Today, if there's a thunderstorm in Chipping Sodbury and no one records it on their phone for Sky News, can we say that it actually happened?

We combine our couch pastimes into 'sit back' and 'sit forward' entertainment. You watch a DVD while sitting back. You update Facebook or play Grand

Theft Auto while sitting forward. The conventional wisdom has it that 'sit forward' entertainment is always better for us, because we are controlling, not controlled, and we are influencing the world as well as being influenced by it.

Up to a point.

This is far too simplistic. Simply acting doesn't mean using discernment, thinking things through, reaching decisions or opening your mind, although it might. Just read the comments of any active blog to see what I mean (or go to www.ifyoulikeitsomuchwhydontyougolivethere.com, the 'spEak You're bRanes' website, which compiles some of blogland's most bizarre postings). Similarly, being passive doesn't mean you're a zombie. There is wonderful, insightful, powerful television everywhere, but you need to use discernment to find it.

Far better than simply being entertained, or being told to perform basically useless actions to entertain ourselves, Russell says, is to 'construct purpose' for ourselves instead. This is not about the 'good old days': some computer games do a terrific job of this, creating immersive, problem-solving narratives. The biggest obstacle to purpose, Russell tells us, is that you can't do this if you 'live a life of distractions'.

For us that means being unable to do something without Tweeting it or being unable to consider an opinion mentally without expressing it. What we often think of as wasted time today would, in Russell's ideal world, be quite the opposite: time for reflection.

HERE'S AN IDEA FOR YOU...

You can be still and active. Sometimes it's impossible to think just because you're being asked to do stuff all the time. If you are worried, fretful or confused, consciously isolate yourself for a few hours. Go to the country and sit on a bench, or turn off the music and lie down. Close the office door and switch off your phone. Don't act, think.

17 EXPLOSIVE DISORDERS

Having dealt with overstimulation as a cause of unhappiness, Russell turns to its inevitable result: fatigue. What he calls nervous fatigue is a major cause of unhappiness – for all of us.

DEFINING IDEA...

Hell is other people.
~ JEAN-PAUL SARTRE

All you commuters out there, does this sound familiar? 'The kind of fatigue that is most serious in the present day in advanced communities is nervous fatigue,' Russell says, due in part to 'the constant presence of strangers... the tendency to view the human race as a nuisance'. Travelling on the underground, he says, provokes 'a general diffused rage against all the strangers'.

Don't think you get off lightly, car drivers. Russell was writing in 1930, when a busy road was one that had a car on it. Today road rage is classified in the US as an official mental disorder, based on (I'm not making this up), 'intermittent explosive disorder'.

If you're a nervous wreck and intermittently exploding, then join the club. But more importantly, leave the club.

We have medicalised 'nervous fatigue' in the years since Russell wrote his book. Today, we call it 'stress'. In 1930, stress was something that described a building in a storm or a shelf with too many books on it, but no one was 'suffering from stress'. As a result, there were few ideas and no prescriptions for reducing it. As an aside, my mother complained of what we now would call stress in the 1960s. She visited her doctor, who advised her to take up smoking.

But Russell would have had no concept of, and no time for, a culture which encouraged us to be helpless in the face of nervous fatigue. We'll get to the meat and potatoes of what he prescribes in later pages, but the essence is that, for most of us, the solution is in our hands – or in our minds.

Let's use road rage as an example. Experts on road rage agree on a major contributor: we simply don't think when we drive. We have unreasonable expectations of how long the journey will take, often based on idealised ideas of driving taken from fantasy rather than bitter experience. We glory in speed, and expect perfect roads, perfect cars and perfect drivers. We internalise our frustrations, unable to turn them off. Research shows that 90% of us think we are better-than-average drivers.

The basic requirement that Russell identified (and modern psychologists agree) for dealing with stress is the ability to reflect calmly. Did the driver who cut you up really do that, or were you going too fast? Are you angry with him, or with yourself for being late again when you know the roads were busy? People are shoving on the bus, which is annoying, but they feel like people are shoving them too.

Without the ability to reflect, you can never begin to conquer stress. You can medicate it away, but you're trapped inside Russell's tube carriage of the mind, with a general diffused rage.

HERE'S AN IDEA FOR YOU...
If you feel helpless rage, take some time to write what you feel. Don't try to justify it or feel ashamed; just be honest about the emotions you experience. Expressing your emotion is the first step to what Russell calls 'hygiene of the nerves'.

18 THINK LESS AND DO MORE

If you are plagued by indecision, stop it, Russell says. You're thinking yourself unhappy.

'Worry can be prevented by a better philosophy of life and a little more mental discipline,' says Russell, making us all feel a bit like a particularly disappointing student.

DEFINING IDEA...

A peacefulness follows any decision, even the wrong one.

~ RITA MAE BROWN, WRITER AND SCREENWRITER

Russell had mental discipline all right. Here is a man who was sent to prison for advocating pacifism, wrote a philosophy book to pass the time and whose philosophical master work, which took almost 400 pages to establish that one plus one equals two, was undermined by Godel's incompleteness theorem – which is two lines long.

He could have been disappointed, bitter and sour. He wasn't. This seems something worth striving for. On the other hand, his solution is somewhat irritating, because it is at once extremely effective and almost impossible.

'The wise man thinks about his troubles only when there is some purpose in doing so,' he explains. 'It is quite possible to shut out the ordinary troubles of ordinary days.' He's not talking about shutting out the worries of serious illness, but he is advocating that it's better to worry about finding the best doctor than to fret about the condition at 2 a.m.

When you have a problem, he explains, you get all the information you can together, weigh it up and come to a decision, then 'do not revise it unless some new fact comes to your knowledge'.

Step two: stop thinking about it. 'Nothing is so exhausting as indecision, and nothing is so futile.'

So there we have it. That's how to stop worrying and learn to love your decisions. Russell used it to cure himself of stage fright. How did he do this? 'I taught myself to feel that it did not matter whether I spoke well or ill, the universe would remain much the same in either case.'

I know what you're thinking: that's easy for him to say. And it was, after he'd used his own medicine on himself. To make this work, he says, you need the following attributes:

1. Humility. You're not very important. You could spontaneously explode on the street tomorrow, and it would merit a few lines in the local paper, unless someone had phone camera footage.

2. Conviction. Your decision is not a provisional outcome, dependent on what the next person you meet says to you.

3. Integrity. Russell assumes that when you decide to do something, you will act consistently, even when that integrity causes you problems. He did.

4. Insight. When you gather the facts it means everything – not just the stuff that supports the decision you emotionally want to make. Often we ignore things we know to be true but would rather not face. We need an openness of mind and a willingness to reconsider that few of us have. But note that this isn't a method to make sure you're correct; just one to make sure you can be happy with what you decide.

HERE'S AN IDEA FOR YOU...

Former prime minister John Major had the habit of making decisions by folding a piece of paper in half lengthwise, and writing arguments in favour on one side, and against on the other. That's a sound way to get all the arguments into your mind.

19 IN TWO MINDS

Russell would set his unconscious mind to work to solve problems for him while he got on with something else. He thinks you can too.

Have you ever woken up and suddenly realised the answer to a problem that you haven't thought about for weeks? Sometimes it's so obvious that you can't imagine how you didn't come across the answer last month when you were fretting about it night and day.

This is no accident, Russell says. He goes further: you can train yourself as a sort of problem-solving machine while you get on with your daily life.

DEFINING IDEA...

Art is a marriage of the conscious and the unconscious.
~ JEAN COCTEAU

When we worry ourselves to sleep with our unsolved problems, we're accustomed to waking up unhappy again, with the problem still stubbornly refusing to yield. And we sleep badly too, so we haven't only failed to solve the problem, but we're also too knackered to solve it, or any other problem, during the day. Eventually we reach a sort of equilibrium where we never truly leave our problems alone and rarely come to any insight. We muddle through, seeking reassurance by copying our emails to everyone, organising conference calls or doing more or less what we did last year.

Russell did the opposite. He was a sort of zen master of mathematics, and ultimately of ethics, when it came to solving complex problems. He thinks, he claims, 'with the greatest intensity of which I am capable for a few hours or days,' in his conscious mind. He then gives orders to his unconscious for 'work to proceed underground', and doesn't think about the problem again for a few months. When he goes looking for the problem in his mental filing cabinet, he often finds that his unconscious has taken it out, solved it and then filed it for him.

Sounds unlikely? We're not accustomed to conceptualising our minds like this. But reflect on this and there are plenty of examples of it happening. If you have ever pulled out a presentation at work that you wrote six months earlier but were unhappy with, and immediately realised the problem with the structure, you've been processing without consciously thinking.

To do this, you need to develop these Russellian attributes:

1. Planning: if you're going to salt your decisions away for a few weeks, you need to start processing early.

2. Intensity: Russell wasn't talking about playing around with the problem. He was talking about using all his faculties to do the initial processing, which should have at least organised the problem and established the work to be done.

3. Discipline: your unconscious can't work if you keep interrupting it. Have the confidence to leave the problem alone.

4. Realism: You can't guarantee a result. Your unconscious processor isn't better than you; it's just you without interruptions and distractions. You might want to delegate really hard stuff to the experts. And even then, there are no guarantees.

But try this; it really does work. And if that fails, organise a conference call.

HERE'S AN IDEA FOR YOU...

If you have to write reports, do academic work or create presentations, get into the habit of making a rough draft a few weeks before you need it. Take time to review it (or send it for comments), identify where it needs to improve – then don't do anything for a few days at least.

20 HOTTIES AND NOTTIES

We all experience envy. But it doesn't just make us unhappy – it also robs us of the capacity for happiness in the future, whatever we do.

'Children are only slightly more open in their expressions of envy… than are grown-up people,' says Russell. 'Take, for example, maid-servants…' No, we're not going to go into the maid-servant anecdote. Why should he have a maid when we have to do everything ourselves? What makes him so special? It's not fair.

'The only cure for envy among ordinary men and women is happiness,' Russell says. Or, put another way, envious people are unhappy by definition.

DEFINING IDEA…

There's nobody in the world like me. I think every decade has an iconic blonde like Marilyn Monroe or Princess Diana and right now, I'm that icon.

~ PARIS HILTON

We all, to some extent, compare ourselves to other people with whom we find some common ground. Russell asks the question 'Have you ever praised an Egyptologist to another Egyptologist?' but, translated into the real world, we've all had the experience of praising someone to a third party, being told we're talking rubbish and realising afterwards that we weren't wrong. We were only hurting the childlike feelings of the person who was listening by not praising them just as much.

Nothing makes us into children and maid-servants as surely as envy. The usual alternative, a polite backing off from praise of anyone in case someone else is hurt, is surely the wrong idea; it's an 'all must have prizes' approach that rounds everything down to a common level of mediocrity. It indulges our inner child.

Russell starts at the opposite end of the problem: if we are one of his Egyptologists, or similar, it is our primary task not to find fault with our peers, but find reasons to admire them. This allows us to discover alternatives to the negative way of comparing ourselves to other people, but without denying the instructive elements of comparison.

This isn't easy, because that's how the media defines its subjects: who is hot and who is not, who is fat and who is thin, who wore a good dress and who wore an ugly one –the emphasis is always on the negative. I wouldn't want to make you watch it, but the high priestess of envy culture, Paris Hilton, acted in a film called *The Hottie and the Nottie*, currently rated on the Internet Movie Database as the fifty-second worst film of all time. You can guess the plot: ugly girl can't get boyfriend, is made over, is beautiful, etc. As an instruction manual in envy, it couldn't be more effective: you're either beautiful on the outside or worthless inside and out.

To avoid the destructive effects of mentally dividing the world into hotties and notties, we can do no better than follow Russell's advice to look to ourselves before criticising others. 'When anything pleasant happens it must be enjoyed to the full,' he says, 'without stopping to think it is not so pleasant as something else.'

HERE'S AN IDEA FOR YOU...

When people have problems, we empathise. The way we describe it is that we 'feel their pain'. But it's just as important to 'feel their pleasure' when they succeed. Think how it would feel: envy limits you, but positive empathy inspires you.

21 NEVER ENOUGH

Don't confuse achievement with happiness. Unless you can conquer envy, you'll never be happy, no matter how much money you have or how important you are.

DEFINING IDEA...

Most people would succeed in small things if they were not troubled with great ambitions.

~ HENRY WADSWORTH LONGFELLOW

The spur that dissatisfaction gives us is the root of ambition. It's the subject of a thousand business books on personal development. If you picked this book up in a bookshop along with another one called *The Ten Secrets of Grinding your Mate's Face in it to Win and be Rich!*, then put that back. It might, possibly, make you rich – but it won't make you happy.

Russell points out in his chapter on envy that outperforming other people can't make you happy in itself. You can't avoid envy by success alone, because there is always someone else more successful to envy. If envy drives you to strive to succeed, it's not simply going to disappear the minute you get a promotion.

We can envy Napoleon, Russell points out, because he was the most powerful man in the world. But Napoleon envied Alexander the Great. And Alexander envied Hercules, 'who never existed', as Russell says. That's setting the bar high.

The root of this unhappiness is our quite natural inability to see the worth of our achievements in isolation. That contented feeling you have when you finish in the gym, complete a hard day of work, even when you wake up and realise it's Saturday, that's a feeling of simple achievement. It doesn't matter if the achievement is running for an hour or making it through the week, it's a simple, personal pleasure.

We have far too few of these feelings that the achievement is sufficient in itself, and is not cheapened by the superior achievements of others any more than it is validated by someone's failure. You're not a better driver because the guy next to you failed the test that you passed. You're not suddenly worse at your job because one person out of fifty candidates got the promotion, and it wasn't you.

So Russell is saying that it's fine to strive, to want to be the best you can be, and to take pride in your achievements. But for him this is a personal quest where you measure up to values you create for yourself – not the values of others. To do that, you have to have a firm idea of what these values are. Many of us simply take the values that we are shown by television and magazines. We overvalue money and celebrity, and undervalue integrity, kindness, trustworthiness or altruism.

Yet if we create a more rounded aspiration for ourselves, we can succeed in our own terms. In this way we can finally escape from the endless staircase of envy, which Napoleon couldn't do. Ultimately he might have envied you. After all, Russell writes, what is more enviable than happiness?

HERE'S AN IDEA FOR YOU...

Don't set your ambition as a goal to reach; instead think of ways you want to live. Ambitions should be paths to follow, not destinations. Being a millionaire by the age of forty has no value if you cheated to win, and are still miserable because you're not a billionaire.

22 LOST IN THE FOREST

At times of hardship, we relish the politics of envy. We may be angry, but blaming other people for what we perceive as injustice cannot make us happier.

DEFINING IDEA...

Not doing more than the average is what keeps the average down.

~ WILLIAM M. WINANS, PREACHER

In the UK, there has recently been a revival of political extremism, much of it directed against immigrants. You don't have to look hard to find the voice of dissatisfied people who have been marinated in envy, and are looking for someone who can right what for them is a perceived injustice. We are, Russell says, all 'lost in the forest'. But it's our responsibility to try to get out of it.

On the one hand, injustices create envy, and Russell does not claim that it is either correct or possible to make that envy go away if the injustices are real. 'As soon as there are seen to be injustices, there is no remedy for the resulting envy except the removal of the injustice,' he writes. Yet this is distinct from the illusion of justice that is created by simply trying to make the envy go away, which is, he says, the 'worst possible kind' of justice.

Why? Because any system of justice that concentrates on diminishing the pleasure of the fortunate rather than increasing the pleasure of the unfortunate is wrong.

This doesn't always hold in real life: people who save money by not insuring their cars, knowing the police are unlikely to find them, are not just fortunate, they're irresponsible. Reducing their pleasure might be appropriate before they plough into the back of your car and write it off.

But it is a general principle that's worth using as a way to stop unhappiness taking hold of us. There's nothing more satisfying then having someone to blame. But what we achieve is a general rounding down, as the most envious person with power pulls everyone into mediocrity.

In Search of Excellence, written by Tom Peters and Robert H. Waterman, has for almost three decades been one of the business books that you can't miss. It sold three million copies in the first four years. Peters had collected forty-three companies that he thought embodied excellence, and wrote a book about why. His idea was to capture the elements of excellence so that others could copy them.

But his motivation wasn't simply to be nice. On the twentieth anniversary of publication, he recalled in an interview that, 'My agenda was this: I was genuinely, deeply, sincerely, and passionately pissed off!' He was annoyed with other management gurus: Peter Drucker, who he said favoured structure too much, and Robert McNamara, the former US Secretary of Defense who had introduced accounting principles into managing a war. The systems that both had created were standard operating practice at the time. But instead of writing articles about how wrong he believed they were, he wrote a book showing how things could be done better, and inspired a new generation of leaders.

HERE'S AN IDEA FOR YOU...

Workplace gossip is rarely about who's done well or deserved their reward. More often it's about who is getting more than you or working less. If you have a problem, take it up with your manager. Practise saying 'It's none of my business' to the people who want to spread poison.

23 BOLLOCKS TO UNHAPPINESS

Russell had no time for the arbitrary sense of sin that society gives us. We'd be happier, he says, if we didn't worry so much about doing things that hurt no one – like swearing.

Having struggled at an early age with the existence, or otherwise, of a god, Russell never wavered from a firm belief that Christianity was not a route to individual happiness. The reason, he suggests, is that it gives us far too much of a sense of our own sinfulness and far too little sense of our own worth.

DEFINING IDEA...

It ain't sin if you crack a few laws now and then, just so long as you don't break any.
– MAE WEST

The idea that we have a conscience, which tells us when we sin, and which promotes a sense of remorse and repentance is, he says, illogical – and makes a lot of things that we do into sources of unhappiness for no practical reason.

Simply, he points out that experience tells us what we call 'conscience' is not universal, and so there can't be a universal arbiter of it.

What we label as conscience, in Russell's opinion, is a mixture of several emotions. Fear of being found out or fear of being an outcast from the group are the two strongest, and if you are tempted to lie for no constructive reason or steal, for example, conscience may be a useful mechanism. But the sense of sin that makes Russell crazy is the one where there's no 'reason visible to introspection' for it. We don't know what we've done wrong, but we know we feel guilty.

So, to swearing. It's arbitrary that we generally feel guilty for saying 'fuck', but can say 'feck' to anyone without worry. It's not that we can't describe the act, because 'shag' also hardly raises an eyebrow. The word 'wanker' is relatively inoffensive in the US, but more offensive in the UK. According to the *Hitchhiker's Guide to the Galaxy*, the most offensive word in the universe is actually 'Belgium'.

Exact statistics vary from country to country (as do the number of taboo words), but in the West the majority of people who speak will swear at times. We do it to express raw emotion, to bond with others, to signal trust or to camouflage our insecurity, but we do it at a price: the feelings of guilt and transgression that go with offending a moral code that we are constantly reminded of. 'This is simply silly,' Russell says, and indeed it might be.

But if other people are offended, should we swear in public? Russell's prescription: swear all you like and don't worry about the words; worry about the feelings of other people. So your great aunt might not like your choice of language, and it would be considerate to moderate it while she's around. But don't feel guilty over your choice of words as a result. It doesn't necessarily mean she has a superior morality to you. It means she chooses to describe her thoughts using different language.

HERE'S AN IDEA FOR YOU...

An accommodation that bilingual people often make is to swear in, say, Spanish when in the UK and English when in Spain. If you want to swear around people who get offended, make up your own swear words; you know what they mean. Everyone's happy.

24 MAKE LOVE, NOT RULES

Russell was a robust champion of sexual freedom. If you enjoy it, he writes, do it.

Russell paints a picture of the sexually unsatisfied housewife, who 'instinctively holds herself back in her relationships with her husband and is afraid of deriving any pleasure from them.' What is she afraid of?

Russell's objection to conventional sexual morality is that it is taught too early, that we are told certain things are wicked when we are too young to fully understand or comprehend them, and that a sense of 'maudlin penitence' which follows means we consider that we 'feel bad, but we don't know why' if we indulge ourselves.

This means that we are unable to make what he would consider rational choices. We veer between denial based on a moral code which is instinctive and imposed and what we consider to be transgressive behaviour, which causes guilt and anxiety rather than pleasure. If we were to say 'It feels so right, but it's wrong,' he would counter, 'in that case, why is it wrong?'

DEFINING IDEA...

I like my sex the way I play basketball, one on one with as little dribbling as possible.

~ LESLIE NIELSEN

He's speaking from a time where sex out of marriage, homosexuality and masturbation were considered sinful by others, but not by him. He doesn't give much weight to the problems of sexually transmitted disease or unwanted pregnancies. Many of us can be rational in what psychologists call a 'cold state', but in the 'hot state' – you don't need an explanation of what that is – we now know that our decision-making processes are very different, and seldom governed by philosophy.

This caveat aside, his central argument still holds good. Worried about having a wank? Why not, if you enjoy it (though check your conditions of employment first if you're in the office)? Would you like your partner to dress up as a police officer? Provided you don't lose the key to the handcuffs, it's nothing to feel guilty about, except when he or she is arresting you.

In the UK we combine a commitment to telling children what is right and wrong with the highest levels of teenage pregnancy in Europe. In the Netherlands, sex education is given as a matter of simple facts: how to use a condom for twelve-year-olds. Teenagers are even taught how to masturbate. A sixteen-year-old understands anal sex. Two twelve-year-olds can consent to have sex. The results are the lowest teenage pregnancy and sexually transmitted disease rates in Europe.

They've followed a model Russell would have liked. 'Until the child is nearing the age of puberty,' he tells us, 'teach him or her no sexual morality whatever.' When you do establish rules, 'Be sure that it is rational, and at every point you can give yourself good grounds for what you say.' Russell was an atheist, so 'it's in the Bible' is not what he was thinking about.

The Dutch model shows that a more open attitude to sexual morality can have beneficial effects. But, eighty years on, as a society we're as far away from Russell's sexual nirvana as ever.

HERE'S AN IDEA FOR YOU...

Guilt about desire shows that one part of you wants things that your conscious mind has decided are wrong. Use the harm principle: if it won't hurt you, your partner, or other people (your partner's partner might be a good example), give it a go. If it doesn't work, it's not shameful.

25 IN VINO VERITAS?

Though he was a big fan of smoking, Russell didn't care for boozers too much – especially the idea that a few drinks help us to see the truth.

We've all been there: after a few drinks we suddenly see the obvious. You need to resign, you really really love your girlfriend and you ought to get married, your best mate is a bastard and needs to be told, it's time to move to Bali and live on the beach.

DEFINING IDEA...

Alcohol is the anaesthesia by which we endure the operation of life.

– GEORGE BERNARD SHAW

These emotions were always risky. Now that you can send a text message or email from your phone, make a 2 a.m. call which sounds perfectly coherent at your end, or book a flight twenty-four hours a day, these moments of apparent clarity can be costly in so many ways. Yet we sentimentally cling to the idea that our drunk selves are what we're really like, that they contain an essence of ourselves that is otherwise unreachable.

This, says Russell, is just lazy thinking – for several reasons.

The first is that we are what we are: if we're different when we're drunk, that's no more the 'real' person than the person we are when we're asleep. 'It is absurd to suppose that moments of weakness give more insight than moments of strength,' Russell says. Instead, being drunk allows you to listen to your unconscious – which is valuable, but not very valuable when your unconscious mind is screaming, 'I want a kebab go on kiss her you're fine to drive he's looking at you funny what's his problem?'

Instead, we should be listening to our unconscious when we have the motor skills and the rational thoughts to integrate it with our lives. If we burst into tears every time we have a glass of wine, we are ducking the responsibility of integrating our needs and desires with our lives. 'Do not be content with an alternation between moments of rationality and moments of irrationality,' Russell adds.

It's not easy. We're very good at keeping the lid on our conscious desires, and our unconscious desires might not be useful. If, when we are drunk, we want to fight with clowns, it doesn't mean we should listen to our unconscious, go to the circus and have a pop when we're sober. Clowns stick together and their big shoes can inflict surprising damage. Integrating might mean training the unconscious mind rather than listening to its orders. Russell is convinced that with discipline and reflection, we can all do this.

You might want a counsellor, you might want to try group therapy or cognitive behavioural therapy if you can't do it yourself. But if you're a difficult, unhappy or crazy drunk, then getting drunk again isn't going to be the answer to what ails you: at best it's an expensive dead end. Russell might underestimate the problems of training the unconscious mind for people less gifted than him, but he's right on the money when he tells us that 'no good was ever done by loss of self-respect'.

HERE'S AN IDEA FOR YOU...

Strong emotion when you're drinking means there are unconscious thoughts trying to break through your resistance. Keep a journal or a diary which holds nothing back. Expressing the thoughts can help to clarify them, and lead you to take action.

26 THEY AREN'T OUT TO GET YOU

Sin is our way of persecuting ourselves, rightly or wrongly. What Russell called 'persecution mania' is the idea that other people are undermining us. But which comes first, the persecutor or our mania?

DEFINING IDEA...

Every sin is the result of a collaboration.

~ STEPHEN CRANE

'We are all familiar with the type of person, woman or man, who, according to his own account, is perpetually the victim of ingratitude, unkindness and treachery,' says Russell. You might be sitting at the opposite desk to one of them now. If you didn't have your nose stuck in this book then they would have been able to finish the job they're doing and would have been able to... well, you know the story.

Some people who consider themselves unlucky present a good story. They almost convince us, until we remember that a similar disaster has happened to them every week for the last three years.

The first point that Russell makes, more politely than I'm about to make it, is that people who are always complaining that everyone's against them are a pain in the arse, and generally speaking don't have many friends. So, broadly speaking, they're correct: everyone does hate them. It's just that they decided this was true, and then made it happen.

How do we know when we're being paranoid, and when they really are out to get us? Russell has some strong medicine for the self-pitying:

1. Don't be a hypocrite. 'We expect everybody else to feel towards us that tender love and profound respect which we feel towards ourselves,' he says. An example: we love to gossip, but we don't like to hear gossip about us.

2. Be consistent in how you assess yourself and others. Friends have faults, but we like them. But it is 'intolerable', Russell says, that they might think the same way about us.

3. Maybe they're not doing this on purpose. If there's a more credible explanation than the idea that everyone is hatching a plot, then that might be the case.

Here's another example. Recently, a friend who was unsure why her boyfriend had not proposed to her decided that it must be because he was already married. She spent time, money and a great deal of emotion uncovering the supposed lies and the pattern of deception that his family and friends were practising. At the end, she was mystified to discover that he wasn't married after all.

It turned out that he hadn't proposed because just wasn't that into her in that way – not surprising, you might think. And if he had the same opinion about his girlfriend as she had about him (the type of person who would use his family to organise a conspiracy to deceive a woman so he could have sex with her) the question isn't 'why hasn't he proposed to me?' but 'why are you even friends?'

HERE'S AN IDEA FOR YOU...

If you feel persecuted by someone, try to imagine the problem without you at the middle of it. Maybe you are just the bystander who got caught up. Either help them to achieve their goal or consciously take yourself out of the crossfire if you can, and you'll be happier as a result.

27 NO EXCUSES

If you consider yourself unlucky, you might just be making your own bad luck.

DEFINING IDEA...

Good luck is another name for tenacity of purpose.
~ RALPH WALDO EMERSON

Humans, because they place themselves at the centre of every event, naturally relate external events to themselves. We're hard-wired to learn from experience and so we personalise that experience, and Russell doesn't try to deny that. But we have been given a faculty to rise above our primitive programming. Using our brains, we can dismiss the things that seem linked, but which have no relationship in reality.

Belief in luck as your saviour is as sure to destroy happiness as any belief you can have. Chance exists: if you flip a coin three times, you may get three heads in a row. That doesn't mean that someone was controlling the coin, or that it's a very significant result (one in eight of you will get it if you try it now). If you win the lottery it wasn't somehow intended for you to do that. In a six-number draw the sequence 1, 2, 3, 4, 5, 6 will win as often as 3, 9, 34, 38, 43, 49. Chance is arbitrary.

How do we minimise the effect of luck on our happiness? Russell talks of 'unlucky' failed inventors, who believe that 'manufacturers are set in their ways. The few who are progressive keep inventors of their own'. The belief offers some comfort, but not a lot.

Mandy Haberman, who invented the Anywayup Cup for toddlers to drink out of, is a successful inventor. But as she points out, if you're an inventor and only success brings happiness, you're not unlucky. You're in the wrong job: 'Only 0.02 per cent of products that are patented get to market... if you're looking to make money, you're better off playing the lottery.'

There's not room for everyone to succeed. You might be having the same experience as thousands of equally deserving cases. If 300 people apply for a job, only one can get it. If the top 10% of performers in your company get a bonus, nine out of ten will not.

So while cause and effect exists, the linkage is often not as solid as we imagine, and it isn't directed at you, or me, or Bertrand Russell. It matters more how we control the things we can control rather than how we react to the things we can't; the sure way to improve your happiness as an inventor is to make a better product.

The world isn't arranged for us. We sometimes don't get what we want. All we can do is use what we have to make the best of what we can be – and have the guts not to blame others when that doesn't succeed.

HERE'S AN IDEA FOR YOU...

Often we use the unpredictability of external events as a reason not to try. Make a plan B and promote a no-excuses culture: success or failure is ultimately your responsibility. Work on ways at work to minimise your exposure to chance.

28 WHAT THEY AREN'T TELLING YOU

We love conspiracies. They excite us, but they also prevent us from becoming happy, fulfilled individuals.

Conspiracy theories didn't begin with the Internet. Russell describes the typical conspiracy-theory wing nut, 1930 version: 'his rebuffs have made such an impression on him that he believes all powerful men to be occupied wholly and solely in covering up the crimes to which they owe their power'.

At the time when Russell was writing, many people in the world believed that 'The Protocols of The Elders of Zion', a fake document which purported to show that a shadowy cabal of Jews was controlling the world's governments, was real. It had been made public in 1905, and among those who believed its veracity were Henry Ford.

DEFINING IDEA...

The biggest conspiracy has always been the fact that there is no conspiracy. Nobody's out to get you. Nobody gives a shit whether you live or die. There, you feel better now?
~ DENNIS MILLER, US COMEDIAN

The 'Protocols' were widely believed for several reasons, one of which was, of course, the widespread anti-Semitism which was present in all levels of society at the time. But it had special resonance in the Depression as many people struggled to find work, as families struggled to feed themselves and as businesses either failed or found it hard to borrow money. At times like this, it is comforting to seek someone or something to blame in a childish way, especially as most of us would predict that we are above average and feel that our natural state, and the only state that will produce happiness, is success. Therefore, when we are unsuccessful we consider that it must be due to some special circumstance or plot.

What is the cure for this persecution mania? Remind yourself, Russell says, that:

1. Your motives aren't always as altruistic as you think they are. Are they undermining you, or frustrating your desire to undermine them? The love of power corrupts us. Russell says, 'The immense majority of even the noblest person's actions have self-regarding motives.' This is good, he adds, in that it gives us zest. But it doesn't make us immune to ethical criticism.

2. Don't overestimate your own merits. Maybe you weren't promoted because you're just not good enough. Don't always look for approval or rage at the lack of it.

3. Don't expect conspirators to be as interested in you as you are in them. You're obsessing over it; they haven't noticed.

4. Don't imagine that people who have something in common, or who have contributed to a situation, have made a plan. There are many people who don't like you, there are many bosses whose actions frustrate you, but it's likely they reached their conclusions independently.

Conspiracy theories, Russell believes, are a flight from the unpleasant truth that we don't mean very much to others or that we're just not good enough. By recognising our deficiencies, we can take pleasure in correcting them, or in finding success elsewhere. By hiding from them and creating imaginary plots, we are condemned to live in fear of monsters that we have created.

HERE'S AN IDEA FOR YOU...

If you think there's a conspiracy afoot, use Occam's Razor, formulated by William of Occam in the fourteenth century. In effect, it says that if there's a complicated explanation and a simple one, the simple one is more likely.

29 IT'S NOT ME, IT'S YOU

Say what you like about Russell, he wasn't a fence-sitter or a flip-flopper. In fact you could have said what you liked about him at any time. Rarely has a man been less bothered by public opinion.

DEFINING IDEA...

The world will only, in the end, follow those who have despised as well as served it.

~ SAMUEL BUTLER, POET

Russell dipped in and out of politics, but he was what we call today a conviction politician: he espoused causes (for example, nuclear disarmament) which he believed in, no matter how unpopular they were, or what the consequences were for his career. He didn't look for arguments, at least not for their own sake; if an argument came his way, he'd have it.

You have the freedom to do this, he says, only if you pay the minimum possible regard to what other people think of you. 'Both in great matters and small ones,' he says, we should respect public opinion 'in so far as it is necessary to avoid starvation and keep out of prison.'

He suggests that indifference to public opinion can be confined to the multitude of mild decisions which we undertake every day. For example, is your car a status symbol, bought to impress others, or the most practical form of transport for you? Are you seeking to impress your friends by holding extravagant dinner parties? Better, he says, to consider travelling or having a good library, which will enrich your experience and give you satisfaction, but perhaps not impress the Joneses as much.

'It is essential to happiness that our way of living should spring from our own deep impulses, and not from the tastes and desires of those who happen to be our neighbours,' he adds.

Russell also extends this to our sexual morality. He points out the inconsistency that adultery, while condemned by most people, is also considered 'excusable if not positively laudable' by the same people in a different social setting. We hold one belief to impress the pious, and another to impress the lads. The result is a tension between two versions of ourselves, which ultimately leads to unhappiness as we subordinate our desires to what society requires of us.

This isn't a charter to do what you want. Imagine you decide that you approve of adultery. It doesn't mean you can have sex with your best mate's partner, because he or she might disagree with your point of view. As might your best mate.

So, you're free to believe what you want. You are free to act on that belief as long as it doesn't land you in trouble or hurt others. Those are your rights. But if you take this road, then you can only achieve happiness if you do it with integrity – that is, if you hold views that spring from considered reflection, not prejudices, your desire for notoriety or because everyone else thinks the opposite. After all, we're not teenagers.

HERE'S AN IDEA FOR YOU...

Imagine you're on your own on an island. What clothes would you have? How many pairs of shoes? How big would your house be? The difference between what you're imagining and what you have now is the stuff you're buying to impress others. Think about this next time you're tempted to splash out.

30 DON'T PANIC

In a crisis we desperately want to make people happy. But if we do this according to what we think they want to hear, we're panicking about panic. We can't be ruled by a fear of rocking the boat.

Public opinion, Russell points out, is always more tyrannical towards those who obviously fear it. He compares it to a dog bullying those who fear it.

Public figures often give the impression that they are guided more by second-guessing how we will react than from their own convictions of right and wrong. If they consider we will tyrannise them we will, but that will often cause the problems they are trying to avoid.

DEFINING IDEA...

Fear cannot be banished, but it can be calm and without panic; it can be mitigated by reason and evaluation.
~ VANNEVAR BUSH, US SCIENTIST

Politicians are not just slaves to shifts in the public mood; they are attuned to recognise it. They are a self-selecting group who are sensitised to what others think of what they do. All of us who seek public approval – at work, in the family, in any organisation where we seek responsibility – suffer the same fear of losing control.

In a crisis, this can have unintended consequences. Risk communication specialist Peter Sandman, an expert on how authorities handle panic, points out that what we perceive as risks are not necessarily what we should be afraid of: 'If you look at a long list of risks, and you rank them in order of how upset people get [about them], then you rank them again in order of how much harm they do, then you correlate the two, you get a glorious 0.2.' A correlation of 0.2 means, in layman's terms, that we worry almost equally about big and small risks, and the risks we worry about most are often relatively minor. We're using criteria other than harm to decide what we fret about.

So, because we're upset about bird flu, knife crime or mercury in our fillings, it doesn't mean this emotion reflects real risk. Gut feel is not a good guide; so when we, as bosses, try to manage this gut feel, we often do the wrong thing.

Sandman defines the feeling that Something Must Be Done as 'Outrage', which doesn't correlate well with 'Hazard'. The problem comes in the many cases of high outrage and low hazard, where, he says, there is a long history of governments making bad decisions due to an oversensitivity to public opinion: 'Official "panic panic" is common. That is, officials often imagine that the public is panicking or about to panic… They withhold information, they over-reassure, they express contempt for public fears…' This 'panic panic', imagining that we're all about to go running around with our hair on fire, not only fails to reassure us, but can have real-world effects on our health or well-being – for example, in flu pandemics.

Give people bad news, but do it responsibly, Sandman says – then other people rarely panic, and are less unhappy than if you try to shield them from the truth. Then you're doing a responsible job of leading. If you're afraid of the angry dog of public opinion, you're just encouraging it to bite you.

HERE'S AN IDEA FOR YOU…

Sandman says an ideal model for leadership in a crisis was Winston Churchill during the Second World War: he didn't try to gloss over problems or avoid hard truths. Next time you are gripped with fear at giving bad news, think 'What would Winston do?'

31 MAN OR MANIPULATOR?

Our fear of what others think creates a desire to manipulate them. *The Conquest of Happiness* **is truly a self-help book, because it tells us the real secret of success is in becoming true to ourselves, not bending others to our will.**

DEFINING IDEA...

Public Opinion... an attempt to organize the ignorance of the community, and to elevate it to the dignity of physical force.
~ OSCAR WILDE

An adolescent who has 'exceptional merit' can often be unhappy, Russell says, because he can't feel comfortable in his environment. Afterwards 'he may find himself throughout his whole life practically compelled to conceal his real tastes and convictions'.

This fear of what people might think needs to be challenged, he says; it leads to the desire to scapegoat others, and also stops us from learning and communicating well with people who are different or come from other cultures. We erroneously learn that difference is threatening, not healthy, and that people aren't here to challenge us, but to be handled and managed.

This attitude has informed many of recent history's 'self-help' books, which are really only self-help in that they are dedicated to achieving a goal. They are all about the end, not the means. Russell would probably have been slightly offended that they sit side-by-side on a shelf with his books, or more likely in front of them.

If you're interested in *Get Laid Now! The Man's Guide to Picking Up Women and Casual Sex*, by Tab Tucker or *The Natural Art of Seduction: Secrets of Success With Women,* by Richard La Ruina ('I have a huge selection of routines and tricks… these things work and I'll teach some to you'), go ahead. They're very successful books, and – like the large selection of books on how to be attractive to men so you can get a husband, or how to impress your boss so you can get a job – they all purport to base their advice on the need to acquire confidence and appear successful and attractive.

It's like asking whether a successful business is one that makes a profit. The answer is that yes, it's one measure of success. If we then seek only to make profits, does the business become more successful? It might be more profitable, but if its employees are miserable and its suppliers exploited, is this truly a success?

We're not businesses, we're people. But if we focus on being successful in the eyes of other people, we can continue to develop that success and maybe we will have more sex, find a rich partner, or get a promotion. We will have helped ourselves by the standards of the society in which we live, and more people whose opinion we don't care about will admire us.

If you're too busy getting stuff for yourself, you might also cry a bit at night because you're lonely, want real love or hate the idea of your job. Manipulating people won't solve those problems.

HERE'S AN IDEA FOR YOU...

There are two types of self-help: the stuff that tells you to be something, and the stuff that helps you to live a more satisfying life. The first is about what you are, the second is about what you do. If you've got a lot of books in the first category, you might want to throw them away.

32 YOU ARE WHAT YOU ARE

Now for the good news: you don't have to be clever, good looking or talented to be happy – but you do need to know yourself.

Having spent half a book describing all the types of unhappiness, and the way in which our habits and customs deny us pleasure, it's frankly a bit of a relief when Russell turns to the causes of happiness. But first he spends some time considering the question that must have occurred to every one of his readers by now: is happiness still possible?

DEFINING IDEA...
The important thing in life is not the triumph but the struggle.
– PIERRE DE COUBERTIN

The question, as phrased by Russell, implies that there was once a state of common bliss, in which we were all innocently happy to live our lives, rather like the animals which Russell approves of. A bit of reflection (disease, hunger, cold and danger make us unhappy, and there have been plenty of all four throughout history), and a quick glance at literature through the ages (from the Old Testament onwards, we are perpetually in a state of decline, even as we get richer, warmer, healthier and crime falls) shows that objectively, we're not badly off. But we're not happy.

'From the conversation and the books of some of my friends I have been almost led to conclude that happiness in the modern world has become an impossibility,' says Russell, who could sound chipper and breezy if he was carving his own gravestone. He, you'll be glad to know, disagrees. His counter-examples include his contented gardener, who was fighting an unwinable war against rabbits: 'of which he speaks exactly as Scotland Yard speaks of Bolsheviks'.

But what if we have university degrees and employees and pension plans and books to finish? It's not the nature of the work or the level of the achievement in the eyes of others, Russell chides us, it's the attitude we bring to it. 'Pleasures of achievement demand difficulties such that beforehand success seems doubtful although in the end it is usually achieved.' An example: you take little pleasure from walking. If one day you were seriously injured and confined to a hospital bed for six months, you would take considerable pleasure from a single step.

The secret of deriving pleasure from your everyday actions, in Russell's view, is to be 'emotionally simple'. This has nothing to do with intellect, but everything to do with honesty. To achieve your goal you need 'a not excessive estimate' of your own powers, but an accurate one. If you are conceited, it may protect you against the disappointment of who you really are, but it will deliver more disappointment as you live and continually fail to match your own estimation of yourself.

Happiness isn't graded so that it's only available to the rich or clever. Next time you sneer at someone and say 'well, as long as he's happy doing that,' remember that at that moment he's happy – and you're not.

HERE'S AN IDEA FOR YOU...
We too easily retreat from challenges because we think we're not good enough. Dig out your sketchpad, your French phrasebook or your gym membership card, and set yourself a goal that's personal – not to please others. Achieving that goal brings pleasure from struggle.

33 LEAVE IT ALL OUT THERE

We naturally work, play and live within ourselves, too scared or too cynical to push ourselves to the limit – and we deny ourselves the possibility of happiness when we do this.

DEFINING IDEA...

Our aspirations are our possibilities.

~ ROBERT BROWNING

Is there joy in work? We live in a world where 'strength through joy' was appropriated by the Nazis, and similar encouragements were used to consign generations of communists in Russia, China and Eastern Europe to backbreaking work. Russell lived in a time when the pleasures of hard work were more associated with great Victorian entrepreneurs than murdering tyrants, and so he takes a more positive view of it than we are accustomed to.

He even takes a few paragraphs to explain how happy the young workers of Russia must be. 'The most intelligent young people in Western countries tend to have that kind of unhappiness that comes of finding no adequate employment for their best talents,' he says, 'the intelligent young at the present day is probably happier in Russia than anywhere else in the world.'

Just you wait, Bertrand.

His point is that by offering others the chance to reach their potential, and by taking it when it is offered to us, we increase not only our happiness but the total sum of happiness in the world. We can take pleasure that there was one Bertrand Russell who drained every last drop of his ability, but pain that there must have been thousands of potential Russells born in India, China, Africa and South America in history who died young or never learned to read.

We can't cure that, but we can diagnose and remedy our own pathology. 'Cynicism such as one finds very frequently among the most highly educated young men and women of the West results from the combination of comfort with powerlessness,' Russell says, and there's a strong argument that this is still true. Powerlessness means that you can't really be bothered, and comfort means you don't mind.

By contrast, since 1999, the number of students in China has been growing at 30% a year. In the last six years the number of graduates has quadrupled. In 2010 there were more PhD engineers and scientists in China than in the US: people who are changing their circumstances and building companies and cities. For Russell, this combination of the ability to make a difference and the restlessness that comes from personal drive is a key to happiness: 'he becomes a reformer or a revolutionary, not a cynic'.

In the West we expect to have our potential realised – but every time we blow off an exam, cheat our way to success or fake achievement, we are taking one step away from what we could be. Our cultures tolerate this and offer us television, shopping, junk food and downloadable porn as alternatives.

If we each accept that rejecting cynicism and an easy life is more likely to produce more happiness in the whole of our lives, we're each taking one step away from underachievement.

HERE'S AN IDEA FOR YOU...

Close your eyes. Imagine you are at a split in the road. At the other end of the downward path is you ten years from now if you spend every day doing the same thing: unhealthy, bored with yourself. An upward path leads to what you could be in ten years if you take those opportunities. Open your eyes, and take the first step on the upward path.

34 ON HAVING A HOBBY

Collecting stamps or snuff boxes, learning to salsa. Hobbies do more than take up your time.

'One of the most eminent of living mathematicians divides his time equally between mathematics and stamp collecting,' Russell writes, in praise of the benefits of having a hobby. You might consider that he's merely doing two of the most boring things imaginable instead of one, but that's just snarky.

DEFINING IDEA...

Politics is my hobby.
Smut is my vocation.
– LARRY FLYNT

Fads and hobbies, Russell believed, are not in themselves a source of fundamental happiness; they have only a small element of achievement and a much larger element of escapism. The world of stamps contains none of the pain of personal relationships or the dread of failure at work. Similarly, any type of collecting – consisting of acquiring, categorising and ordering for your benefit – is often an escape from the complexity and disappointment of our lives rather than any kind of remedy for it.

But that's not to say that hobbies are a waste of time. 'A friendly interest in things,' Russell tells us, is an important way to create the conditions in which happiness can grow. The mathematician needed a diversion when he was stuck in his day job, one which would yield when the theory of numbers wasn't giving up its secrets. He describes meeting a great writer who he expected to be a miserable bore (I paraphrase) but he turned out to be extremely animated and excited by the baseball results. Russell's conclusion? 'Any pleasure that does no harm to other people is to be valued.'

Another reason to value hobbies is the time they give us for positive reflection. Categorising stamps and ordering them might be a way to try to impose order when that order is denied you in the everyday life you lead, or it might help you to impose order on your thoughts. Russell said that he 'collected rivers' by visiting them. You get a sense that this was a way in which a man who spent a lot of time inside his own head could connect with the outside world and explore other cultures and ideas, even as he floated past them.

Remember also Russell's advice on how to solve a problem: by ordering it, then burying it in your unconscious for the brain to work on it. If you need a distraction while that work goes on, something that occupies your attention without taxing your mind too much is perfect.

Hobbies impose time away from the constant transactional nature of the world. In this they are a good model for friendship. The time you spend with friends having a drink, sharing a joke, watching football, sitting and sharing, captures the nature of a hobby (indeed, can be an aspect of it). It also vastly expands the opportunities for pleasure and personal growth, simply because there is no goal except mutual pleasure.

'Our own powers are limited,' Russell writes. 'If all our happiness is bound up in our personal circumstances it is difficult not to demand more of life than it has to give.'

HERE'S AN IDEA FOR YOU...

We often lose our hobbies because we undervalue them. Schedule them: Thursday night is poker night, or Monday is your dance class. They aren't things to do when you've exhausted all the other possibilities; they have a value of their own.

35 THE JOY OF APPETITE

The way we enjoy food, literally or metaphorically, is an indicator of happiness.

Russell singles out five possible ways to eat. You might be the sort of person who finds all food tiresome – similar to the Byronically unhappy people we met in earlier chapters. You might find a food a duty: it's a necessary evil.

DEFINING IDEA...
Never eat more than you can lift.
~ MISS PIGGY

You might be an epicure, for whom food's never good enough, and is a source of dissatisfaction. Many of you will have been in a restaurant with someone who can't wait to tell you that the food isn't as good as it is somewhere else (often that person's house) to the extent that you're tempted to say, 'Well, go there then and stop ruining our meal.'

Fourth, there's the gourmandiser, who can't stand to have appetite.

Finally, there are the people we aspire to be: happy people who have anticipation and appetite, who can take pleasure in simple food, who want to eat but not stuff themselves. This, he concludes, is a zestful life – but one which many treat with contempt.

It doesn't matter if you like strawberries or not, as long as you eat them if you do like them, don't eat them if you don't, and don't criticise people who don't agree with you. In the same way it's not morally superior to like, or not to like, football, or to think that TV is better or worse than reading a book.

Russell's not really talking about how we eat here, he's talking about our appetite. For example, he discusses how we holiday (or how we travelled in

1930, which sounds very much like the way we travel today). Many travellers, he says, concentrate on eating the same food as at home, socialising with the same people, and find it a relief to be back at home – where, arguably, they should have stayed.

Zest for life, in Russell's model, is the engine of happiness and a system for engaging with the world. It's a way of communicating without putting a filter in front of yourself, an attitude, a front.

You need only meet the women who were the proprietors of boarding houses he visited, Russell says, to see how the desire to criticise others evolves into a disapproving lack of openness and zest. We can sympathise every time we check into a B&B and are met with a long list of rules and prohibitions from a proprietor who forgot long ago that it is better to encourage our appetite for pleasure without contempt. It's hard to work out what they were disapproving of in a middle-aged, titled, English mathematician and philosopher. 'You up there doing your equations again, Mr Russell? The neighbours are complaining that your pencil's too loud!'

HERE'S AN IDEA FOR YOU...

Do the rules you impose on yourself spoil your zest? Start with food. Go somewhere you've never been. Order pudding first if you want it – don't deny yourself and then eat off someone else's plate. Leave the car at home and have a drink. Go on, enjoy yourself.

36 TOO MUCH OF A GOOD THING

Food, dieting, sex, gambling, gyms, video games, chocolate, caffeine: the list of modern addictions is an indictment of how we have become gluttons for pleasure.

Epicurus, the philosopher whose name is now traduced to describe overindulgence, was in fact nothing like the caricature that bears his name. He preferred to drink water to wine, liked plain food and was simply dedicated to happiness. In many ways, his idea of a good life was not so far from Russell's.

DEFINING IDEA...

The most valuable of all talents is that of never using two words when one will do.

~ THOMAS JEFFERSON

He is, though, associated with overindulgence and compulsive consumption – perhaps because this is the behaviour we commonly associate with pleasure. When we enter the lottery, we don't dream of winning one of the minor prizes. Dream cars are fast, noisy and brash. Dream holidays are so stuffed with luxury that we forget where we live. 'Living the dream' does not mean what Epicurus would have associated with pleasure.

It is no surprise that Western communities are prone to addiction. We have both the leisure and the means to pursue addictions that previously were unavailable. Gambling is available for all British adults in the comfort of their own home; an increasingly sexualised culture gives inspirations and outlets for those who compulsively overindulge; kids have the liberty and the opportunity to play computer games until they become a compulsion.

It's not really our place to attempt to unravel what are complex, serious and difficult compulsions. But Russell warns us against sentimentalising all compulsions, or finding a kind of reckless nobility in them. 'The ancients... regarded moderation as one of the essential virtues,' he points out. Where did we go so wrong? Part of the problem, he says, was the Romantic ideal that 'overmastering passions were admired'.

How do we measure moderation? Russell's formula is that our indulgences must be 'compatible with health, with the affection of those whom we love, and with the respect of the society in which we live'.

Russell uses the compulsion to play chess as an example – not one that many of us will be wrestling with – but imagine he's talking about online poker. If you look forward to playing all day you are 'fortunate', he says, but 'the man who gives up work in order to play chess all day has lost the virtue of moderation'.

This further raises the question of the compulsion to follow a dream, to give up a comfortable situation to pursue an obsession. Again Russell makes a distinction: if you have a higher ideal, go for it. If you're merely seeking stimulation, it's ultimately indulgence. He wasn't a mountain climber.

Drawing the line between indulgence – which merely shows you have zest which isn't satisfied by your ordinary life and is a healthy outlet for energy – and overindulgence isn't easy. Following a romantic desire to overindulge isn't useful.

HERE'S AN IDEA FOR YOU...

Addictive behaviour sneaks up on us. Do you lie to others habitually about what you are doing? When you are doing something else, do you constantly find yourself wishing you were doing whatever activity you are denying yourself? If so, you may have a problem, and perhaps you should seek help.

37 NOT JUST A TALKING HEAD

Surrounding yourself with people for whom you have contempt makes you feel superior. Surrounding yourself with people who inspire you gives you joy.

DEFINING IDEA...

Sometimes it's a form of love just to talk to somebody that you have nothing in common with and still be fascinated by their presence.

~ DAVID BYRNE

A few months ago, maybe unconsciously prompted by the spirit of Bertrand Russell, I noticed a copy of *Stop Making Sense* in a pile of slightly dusty DVDs at home. For those of you who missed the 1980s, and there were good reasons to do so, *Stop Making Sense* was a 1984 concert film by the band Talking Heads, inspired and created by the group's presiding genius, David Byrne.

Many people know the film from its final moments, when Byrne dons a giant suit for the closing songs and sings himself into a frenzy while looking like Marlon Brando meets the pinheads. For this, and many other ideas, he has acquired a reputation as a sort of musical clown.

Watching the film again, nothing could be further from the truth. What matters to Byrne – and the people working with him – isn't the destination, it's the joy of the journey. The need to produce what we have to call 'content' today quickly drains the shallow pool of talent for mediocre recording artists, who burst into our consciousness half-formed with three good songs and a CD of fillers, and who three years later are making a difficult third album about how unpleasant it is to be famous and what it's like to sit in a recording studio.

Byrne has never done that, because he has always looked outwards for inspiration. In 1978 he was playing some of the most innovative New Wave music in New York. Three years later he was touring the world with an expanded band which fused the greatest funk musicians of the day and songs produced by Brian Eno. Byrne has a weak voice and dances like a broken puppet, but he can find and merge great creative talent in the search for things that hadn't been done before. He scored operas and wrote brass band music. In 2008 he converted a building into a giant musical instrument.

It is no coincidence that *True Stories*, the film that Byrne wrote and directed in 1986, was the story of the goodness, decency and unnoticed depth of ordinary people like us, told from the point of view of someone who is genuinely interested in what he sees.

We can't all be David Byrnes. There's a strong argument that the world would be insufferable if we were. But just as he surrounded himself with great talent such as Eno, the choreographer Twyla Tharp and the composer Philip Glass, and so has never stopped learning or become stale, we can resist the temptation to surround ourselves with people we despise because it makes us look good.

Look Byrne up on YouTube, and you'll see that he is the living proof of Russell's assertion that hunger is to food as zest is to life.

HERE'S AN IDEA FOR YOU...

If you have a book, a song, even a presentation that you care about, don't just show it to people who will tell you how wonderful you are. Ask someone whose talent you admire to see it, encourage them to be honest, and take their involved criticism as a compliment.

38 NO ONE LIKES ME

Why am I not loved more? We all desire affection, but how far should we go to inspire it in others?

DEFINING IDEA...

Being deeply loved by someone gives you strength, while loving someone deeply gives you courage.

~ LAO TZU

If you're unloved, Russell writes, you may start musing on why you are so dreadful. This introspection, like much fruitless introspection, doesn't impress him much: it doesn't help the person who lacks love, and it doesn't change the situation (few people are inspired to give genuine love to a person who suddenly starts sitting at home worrying).

What matters is what can be done to make us more loved, and for that love to be the type that makes us happier. It's not an easy problem to solve.

Can we bribe people to love us? When I was at school, our class bully became so hateful at one time that even a group of thirteen-year-olds took a stand against him. For a while he wasn't invited to join in, wasn't included in conversations.

After a few days, he brought us sweets, and offered us each a single cola cube to show how he was really a pleasant and easy-going friend. But did we, united in group rejection of everything he stood for, take the gift?

Of course we did. These were free sweets.

Don't worry too much about accepting the gift, Russell tells us. It changes very little. 'Human nature is so constructed that it gives affection most readily to those who seem least to demand it. The man, therefore, who endeavours to purchase affection by benevolent actions, becomes disillusioned by experience of human ingratitude.' So the school bully still lacked affection. The only change was that he, for the first time, had acknowledged that this made some difference to his sense of well-being.

We all try to give presents to win affection. Auction house eBay surveys Christmas spending, and in 2008 it was £368 per person. That's around £23 per present. We work, on average, for one week every year solely to buy presents at Christmas.

Not all these presents are for buying affection but, if we follow Russell's advice, we're wasting the proportion that is. The giver hates ingratitude, but 'it never occurs to him that the affection which he is trying to buy is of far more value than the material benefits which he offers as its price'. In short, you spent £23. You're asking for a lifetime of affection in return from me. If it's a transaction, you're getting the best of that bargain by a long way, so don't be surprised (or even that disappointed) if I don't keep up my end of the deal.

In Russell's view, affection is literally priceless. When we are most needy or when we attempt to buy affection, we become most unattractive, and rightly so. The sense of security that enables you to win and keep affection, he says, is similar to the confidence of a man walking on a narrow plank above a chasm: you are more likely to fall into the abyss if you think that's what is likely to happen.

HERE'S AN IDEA FOR YOU...

The greatest gift you can give a friend is intimacy, involvement with your friend's successes and problems. Prioritise your intimate friends. You can't be involved with all of your 723 Facebook friends, and sending them a virtual hamburger is no substitute.

39 TOO MUCH, TOO YOUNG

It's not loving to seek to please your kids or your partner if the cost to you is unreasonable.

'General self-confidence towards life comes more than anything else from being accustomed to receive as much of the right sort of affection as one has need for,' Russell tells us. He points out that this affection begins, as a child, with the special bond between parent and child. 'The child from whom, for any reason, parental affection is withdrawn is likely to become timid and unadventurous, filled with fears and self-pity, and unable to meet the world in a mood of gay exploration.'

Part of this is because the world, a 'higgledy-piggledy place', will present us with both good and bad things if we choose to explore it. If we are too preoccupied with approval and comfort, setbacks are disastrous – if we choose to risk them at all.

DEFINING IDEA...

You can learn many things from children. How much patience you have, for instance.
~ FRANKLIN P. JONES, AMERICAN BUSINESSMAN

How much affection is too much? When we give affection, we're not seeking the approval of our children; we're attempting to help them to grow, to support them by using words like 'no'. If they begin to associate a reasonable refusal with disastrous emotional rejection, then when their parents are no longer present they may do everything possible to avoid those feelings of rejection by avoiding any conflict. But even if we can manipulate our parents we can't control the entire world, and those rejections will become as disastrous as they are inevitable.

So here's a Russellist injunction to overprotective mothers: 'The timid mother or nurse, who is perpetually warning children against disasters that may occur, who thinks that every dog will bite and every cow is a bull, may produce a timidity in them equal to her own.'

And, for the grown man who cannot come to terms with the fact that he is not a child any more: 'They seek from their wives what they obtained formerly from an unwise mother, and yet they are surprised if their wives regard them as grown-up children.'

A thought on this: we often use the term 'Stepford Wife' (based on the novel by Ira Levin in which wives are replaced by identical robots) as a term of abuse for a wife who is totally and unreasonably dedicated to the happiness of her husband. Yet the main target of the original book are the Stepford men, who are seemingly unable to be married to women who are not totally dedicated to their pleasure and satisfaction. When we make fun of a Stepford couple that we know, we shouldn't spend our time solely criticising the wife. Maybe we should be asking if the husband finds the alternative – marriage to someone who is free to disapprove of him – unbearable.

HERE'S AN IDEA FOR YOU...

Don't let the 'but Dave's mum lets him do it' reason trump everything when your kids try it on. Don't measure what's right by what your immediate society thinks is right. Long after Dave's mum has forgotten you ever existed, you'll still be responsible for the happiness of your children.

40 BADGE KISSERS

Affectionate loyalty is a gift, not a business deal. If you treat it as a transaction it diminishes the happiness of everyone involved.

Every summer it's the same: the footballers who have spent the last ten months pledging their lifelong loyalty to their club, its fans and their team-mates swap clubs, say it has always been a dream to play for their new club, and pledge their lifelong loyalty, etc.

DEFINING IDEA...
Fidelity purchased with money, money can destroy.
– SENECA

What they're really pledging loyalty to, in most cases, is the increased wage they have been promised. As they pass from one country to another, from one league to another, their lifelong, or at least career-long, loyalties are to the people who put that in front of them: the agents, the sports management companies, the sponsors and the lawyers who will follow them.

Football fans have a derisive term for a player whose overstated loyalty to the club means they will never leave: badge kissers. One of the funniest in recent history was Ashley Cole, whose laugh-out-loud ridiculous autobiography told us that, 'My heart and soul was tied to Arsenal with a fisherman's knot. I don't think even Houdini could have unravelled it.' Then Arsenal offered him only £55,000 a week wages in his new contract, and he signed for Chelsea.

We're none of us surprised that affection is a tradable commodity in football, but our motivations in bestowing affection on our friends are also often suspect. Russell explains that if our motivation for giving (or enjoying) affection is not what we claim it to be, we cannot be happy.

Imagine you are on a boat, cruising down the coast, he says. You look with affection at the coastline. Then the boat sinks, and you find yourself looking with affection at the coastline once more, but this time with the affection of a drowning man swimming to the shore.

The difference is that the first affection comes from a position of confidence and safety. The second comes from fear. It's self-centred.

Translate this into our everyday lives. We express affection and allegiance for many groups: family, friends, colleagues, even football clubs. In all of those there's a mixture of security – where, according to Russell's analysis, the affection, freely and lovingly bestowed, adds zest – and insecurity, where we are like drowning men swimming for the shore. The affection in this case is based on what we can take. It adds fear. It's not, ultimately, a happy relationship.

If we bestow affection only because of what we are getting out of the deal, it's not really affection. We'll either be disappointed if we don't get what we were expecting, or if we discover that the other party is doing the same and they got a better offer – metaphorically, a bigger club came in for them.

Loyal affection that inspires happiness in us and others is a gift. In that way, it is brave. 'Of all forms of caution, caution in love is perhaps the most fatal to true happiness,' Russell says.

HERE'S AN IDEA FOR YOU...

It's easy to become transactional in all our relationships. 'I'll do this if you do that,' can be benign in small doses, but if you feel it changing to 'I'm not doing this because you don't do that,' then it might be time to find a new friend, job or partner.

41 HAVING IT ALL

Should you have children? Russell warns against lazily assuming children will replace the fulfilling life you give up.

DEFINING IDEA...

That's the key to having it all: stop expecting it to look like what you thought it was going to look like.

– CINDY CHUPACK, SEX AND THE CITY

The relations between parents and children, Russell says, 'are, in nine cases out of ten, a source of unhappiness to both parties, and in ninety-nine cases out of one hundred a source of unhappiness to at least one of the parties'. As the spoof newspaper *The Onion* reported in 2007 when it carried a (fictitious) report that 95% of US parents abused their children: '…it documents abuses ranging from less severe offenses, such as children being denied snacks just before dinner, to more egregious, long-term causes of neglect such as never getting what they want, ever'.

We can't control the emotions of hormonal children; but we can control whether we have the rugrats in the first place. Russell provides an analysis of the modern mother's dilemma which has changed little since 1930: what do you do if you like your life as it is, but really want a child?

The current fashion is to claim that you can 'have it all', though this seems more designed to make ordinary people feel inferior to the supermums covered in the press than to reflect the situation in reality.

Instead, as Russell points out, a single working woman has her own income and status, comfort, and stimulation to be interesting. Motherhood tends to remove at least some of this: 'She becomes tied to her house, compelled to perform herself a thousand trivial tasks quite unworthy of her ability and training… she is fortunate indeed if she does not soon lose all her charm and three quarters of her intelligence… the woman who talks about her day-time troubles is a bore, and the woman who does not is absent-minded.' Sorry to tell you this if you're trying for a baby. I'm sure it won't be quite like that.

What can you do to maximise your happiness? Russell didn't try to dismiss the special bond between parents and children but, he says, don't be pressured into sacrificing your whole life for a child, simply because society tells you it's the right thing.

If this sounds cold, he doesn't mean it to be. His logic is that the bond between parents and child is mutually satisfying and so a useful source of happiness: 'Parenthood is psychologically capable of providing the greatest and most enduring happiness that life has to offer,' he says. If it weren't for this mutual emotional bond, he implies, there's really no point.

Russell advocates having kids – 'When circumstances lead men and women to forego this happiness, a very deep need remains unsatisfied' – but he doesn't espouse the vogue for dedicating your lives to them when it comes at the expense of your own fulfilment. This is especially true if you were happy when you were childless.

HERE'S AN IDEA FOR YOU…
When your time is stretched as a parent it's easy to fall into a habit of only taking time out for necessities: going to the supermarket or cooking a meal. Scheduling time for yourself can help you remember who you are and do what makes you happy.

42 POWER AND TENDERNESS

The conflict between parents and children, Russell believed, has its root in our desire to be loving – but also in our joy in the power we have over a helpless human.

Babies are rubbish at cooking a full English breakfast. Ask your six-year-old daughter to climb on the roof and adjust a satellite dish, and you'll never hear the end of the complaining. And frankly, when you see the feeble attempts of primary school children to change a tyre, you realise why mechanics aren't cutting their prices because of the competition.

DEFINING IDEA...

The real menace in dealing with a five-year-old is that in no time at all you begin to sound like a five-year-old.

– JEAN KERR, HUMORIST AND PLAYWRIGHT

Small people, Russell rightly points out, need their parents. 'There is an intimate blend of power and tenderness. The new creature is helpless, and there is an impulse to supply its needs, an impulse which gratifies not only the parent's love towards the child,' he says, adding: 'but also the parent's desire for power… From an early age there comes to be a conflict between love of parental power and desire for the child's good.'

But this is not unnatural, or necessarily a cause of unhappiness. Babies, with their little bobbly heads and need for clean nappies, aren't in a position to turn down a little help. It puts pressure on us to give the right type of help, and Russell's fear, based in part on his childhood, is that we dishonestly dress up love of power as healthy discipline.

His ally in this is Dr Benjamin Spock who had still not published *The Common Sense Book of Baby and Child Care* when Russell was writing. Dr Spock never advocated permissiveness or abdicating responsibility to your child. He didn't believe that babies found their own way any more than he believed they could cook an English breakfast. He did, however, bring to an end a long tradition of rearing babies through the sort of behavioural methods scientists use to train rats.

Dr Spock's most-remembered innovation was that when your baby cries, you should comfort it. This appears common sense today – but fifty years ago it was accepted that you let the baby cry because, being a little animal, you trained it by not rewarding its cries for help.

Russell suggests we separate the exercise of discipline because it will make our child happier and more able to succeed in the world (positive) from the exercise of discipline Because We Are Your Parents (negative): 'The child should as soon as possible learn to be independent in as many ways as possible, which is unpleasant to the power impulse in a parent,' he says.

Ultimately, tyrannical parents will always fail. Our beloved little monsters have their revenge. They grow up – often, as Russell says, the complete opposite of what we expected.

HERE'S AN IDEA FOR YOU...

As early as possible, get into the habit of explaining why you are doing what you do – as much for your benefit (what is your motivation?) as for the child's. As soon as your kids get the corresponding habit of saying 'but why?' the practice will come in handy.

43 YOU NEVER CALL

The ingratitude! We could be dead, and they wouldn't know. Is it our kids that make us unhappy, or our thwarted selfishness?

Light bulb jokes, a small but significant contribution to the conquest of happiness, post-date Bertrand Russell. At least, he doesn't tell one in any of his recorded speeches and radio broadcasts.

This one isn't in his book:

'How many mothers does it take to change a light bulb?'

'Don't worry, I'll just sit here alone in the dark.'

DEFINING IDEA...

Humans are the only animals that have children on purpose with the exception of guppies, who like to eat theirs.

~ P.J. O'ROURKE

If we enjoy the power that we exercise over our kids, and we exercise that power to excess rather than to achieve mutual happiness, it will follow that we develop a habit of selfishness: we object to our children's independence not because it might lead them into trouble (a common cover story), but because it diminishes our pleasure in using our child to define our own importance.

For Russell the possibility for mothers to resume their old lives, if their previous lives gave them happiness, is not just an option – it's almost mandatory for long-term happiness. In 1930 he was recommending that women had the same right to return to work, and obtain the same benefit from it, as men.

'A woman who has acquired any kind of professional skill ought, both for her own sake and for that of the community, be free to continue to exercise this skill in spite of motherhood... Whenever society demands of a mother sacrifices to her child which go beyond reason, the mother, if she is not unusually saintly, will expect from her child compensations exceeding those she has a right to expect.'

In effect, he's saying that the teenage argument against parental discipline of 'I didn't ask to be born' has some value. The child was not the arbiter of the sacrifices you chose to make when your child was a baby, so it's simply self-indulgence to use them as a bargaining chip in later life.

This is making your blood boil, isn't it? Try this: 'The mother who is conventionally called self-sacrificing is, in a great majority of cases, exceptionally selfish towards her children,' he says.

Russell wasn't suggesting you either dump the kids in nursery and go off to be a stockbroker or you're a bad mother. He's saying that the pressure of society that all mothers should be excellent at mothering is unrealistic, so it's not a defeat to hand over some of it to a professional. And even when he was writing, he didn't see why mothers should sacrifice their entire lives for children, while fathers experienced children as a break in their routine.

'The relation of the mother to the child will have in future to resemble more and more that which at present the father has,' he concludes, 'if women's lives are to be freed from unnecessary slavery.'

HERE'S AN IDEA FOR YOU...

As long as you know the parents and the other children involved, sleepovers are a great way for children to socialise and for you to learn to let go occasionally. Join the Giant Sleepover (www.giantsleepover.com), which organises sleepovers in all sorts of places once a year. You can raise money for charity as well as help your kids.

44 IN DEFENCE OF CALL CENTRES

We can't all have jobs we love. How do we get ourselves through the day?

Russell admits that while it's good to enjoy your work, not many of us actually do. Yet still he lists work as a cause of happiness. Why?

DEFINING IDEA...

We make a living by what we get, but we make a life by what we give.

– WINSTON CHURCHILL

Well let's establish the premise first. The most reliable data for whether people enjoy their work comes from the US, where a company called The Conference Board has been measuring job satisfaction for twenty years. The last time it did the survey, less than half said they were satisfied with their jobs. That's the lowest score for twenty years. Fewer than two in five people under the age of twenty-five were satisfied in their jobs.

If work was a horse, they'd shoot it.

It's seems ridiculous that dull work, your dull work, can be a cause of happiness. Russell notes that even if it is not a cause of great happiness at least it reduces our level of unhappiness: 'Even the dullest work is to most people less painful than idleness… most of the work that most people have to do is not in itself interesting, but even such work has certain great advantages.'

At this point, you must accept that Russell had not, to the best of our knowledge, had experience butchering battery hens or working in a call centre.

The first advantage, he says, is that it gives us something to do. If we're given free choice, every day, most of us don't find anything interesting to do, and we don't tend to get happier – just more bored.

For many of us work provides a place to go and a set of friends when we get there. Work might not be much of a job, but it's a place with a ready-made social life that would be tough to create if we had to do so from scratch.

Working, he also says, makes our holidays better. Though also, I must point out, shorter.

He does offer some more tangible results of a dreary job. The first is that it gives us money. Money isn't happiness, but it certainly doesn't hurt. Work satisfies our need for ambition and desire to strive. Even if your status brings little money and no significant let-up in the tedium, it can also bring a reputation and skill at your job. Don't take these too lightly, he counsels. To be recognised for your ability in any job offers the chance of happiness.

Pity, then, the job which Russell sees as potentially the most tedious, dead-end work you could hope for: 'The domesticated wife does not receive wages, has no means of bettering herself, is taken for granted by her husband... and is valued by him not for her housework but for quite other qualities.' When he puts it like that, a call centre doesn't seem such an unhappy place.

HERE'S AN IDEA FOR YOU...
If getting through the week is the limit of your ambition at work, maybe the answer isn't a new job, but new responsibilities in the one you have already. Is there anything else you could do, even if it's just organising a regular trip to the pub for your workmates?

45 LIFELONG LEARNING

The best jobs, in Russell's view, are the ones that offer the chance to keep learning. When it's not provided for us, we need to grab it for ourselves.

DEFINING IDEA...

Choose a job you love, and you will never have to work a day in your life.
– CONFUCIUS

Having dealt with the majority who don't like their jobs, let's spend a bit of time working out why people who like their jobs seem to enjoy them.

There are two reasons that Russell can see, and the first is that these jobs give you the chance to acquire and practice skill.

We like acquiring and using skills, Russell says: 'A boy who can stand on his head becomes reluctant to stand on his feet.'

The practice of a skill gives us great satisfaction. Sometimes the skill is competitive; if you're a lawyer or a politician, then your skill is getting the better of someone just like you, someone who is your competition.

Then there is the simple acquisition of skill because it makes us happy to do difficult things: 'A man who can do stunts in an aeroplane… derives satisfaction from the exquisite precision of his operations.' And, perhaps, from the terrified screams of 350 holidaymakers sitting behind him.

The skill doesn't have to be well paid or highly valued by society outside our profession, either. Russell has even heard of plumbers in the same category, though one assumes that his maid actually dealt with them.

But, for any skill to continue giving pleasure, it has to either change, or be possible to improve. Lawyers and politicians can continue up the ladder for many years, but usually our job isn't going to teach us more after a certain time.

What do we do then? We can switch back into the dull-but-employed category, or we can push on and develop new skills. The government calculates that presenteeism – where we show up for work but aren't productive – costs the UK around £900 million per year, but it's mostly a cost that's hidden inside ourselves. We could argue (Russell certainly would) that the much greater cost is in the loss of zest for life that we experience.

We take pleasure in being good at what we're good at, but those gains are constantly eroded. The job itself can change: new products, new structures, new ideas and new technology undermine our hard-earned skills. Economic trends devalue our work; some jobs are being 'de-skilled', others are outsourced, and more are combined to be done in a mediocre way by teams who are guided more by efficiencies of scale than the desire for excellence.

Lifelong learning isn't easy. If your employer will not help you, it might mean taking one step back to take two forward. It will certainly mean some financial hardship if you need to take time off work. But for most of us a single skill cannot provide a career of satisfaction any more.

HERE'S AN IDEA FOR YOU...

If you want to train but are worried abut funding, UK citizens can get Career Development Loans up to £8,000 from three high street banks. While you are training, the government's Learning and Skills Council will pay the interest on your loan, and for one month afterwards. Look at www.direct. gov.uk/cdl for more information.

46 A HIGHER PURPOSE

The most satisfying work has all the components of work with which we are familiar, but to deliver true happiness, Russell says, it must be constructive. Can you say that?

DEFINING IDEA...

You'll always be an artist.
You have no choice.
~ RAPHAEL, IN THE AGONY AND
THE ECSTASY

Michelangelo, Russell admits, isn't the best role model for demonstrating that a constructive purpose promotes happiness. 'Michelangelo maintained... that he would not have troubled to produce works of art if he had not had to pay the debts of his impecunious relations.' They left that bit out of Charlton Heston's script in *The Agony and the Ecstasy*, but the film's title gets over what Russell is trying to say very well. Though the great artist, like his contemporaries, was a slave to patrons such as Rex Harrison (Pope Julius), the work provided them with the ecstasy which ultimately left them satisfied.

Michelangelo might not have been a happy artist, Russell says, but without his great work he'd probably have been even less happy: 'We cannot maintain that even the greatest work must make a man happy; we can only maintain that it must make him less unhappy.'

The can't-fail method for boosting happiness, no matter what the hardship we endure in our work, is that it has a purpose of constructiveness, Russell tells us, contrasting this type of work with the life of the journalist who doesn't believe in the policy of the paper he or she works for, but does it anyway because it's a paying job. Russell says the contrast makes the journalist cynical, and removes all pleasure from the achievement that he or she has from his or her work. This is not universally true, in my experience. At least 50% took the job because they were depressed and cynical already.

What constitutes constructiveness? It doesn't have to be the roof of the Sistine chapel, but it does have to be something that acts as a 'monument' once the work is completed.

We are all motivated by making a difference in more walks of life than we realise: currently the fad among companies is to build 'communities' of enthusiasts for their products, whose advice is sought through bulletin boards and online networks. At first, researchers thought that love of the product or brand was the deciding factor, but what gets them to stay is the knowledge that their input is being recognised and taken seriously. For an example, look up Dell IdeaStorm (www.ideastorm.com), the online community where products are discussed – and where 350 customer ideas have already been implemented.

Great men, Russell says, are ultimately motivated by creating order out of chaos, just as we might be motivated by helping to build a better laptop. Who can he hold up as a model of constructive purpose? 'Those few statesmen who have devoted their lives to producing order out of chaos, of whom Lenin is the supreme type in our day…'

Oh, well, you can't win 'em all.

HERE'S AN IDEA FOR YOU...

We all struggle to believe we make a difference. Where among all the positive achievements in your life, if you hadn't existed, would it have been necessary to invent you? Apply this to your work, your friends, your home. That should make you happy – or at any rate, less unhappy.

47 THE PRICE OF OBSESSION

All work and no play means that you're unlikely to make a good politician – or a happy person.

Denis Healey famously said that Margaret Thatcher's problem was that she had 'no hinterland'. In 2008 he expanded on what he meant by a hinterland: 'knowing the history of things'.

DEFINING IDEA...

My father taught me to work;
he did not teach me to love it.
– ABRAHAM LINCOLN

Jonny Wilkinson, one of our greatest rugby players, was arguably last great in 2003. Since then he has been almost permanently injured, leading to months out of the game, continuous rehabilitation, boredom and disappointment. But a man formerly famous only for his total dedication to kicking an oval ball between some posts has spent his rehab time studying French and Spanish, guitar and piano, physics and Buddhism.

Russell, in writing about the pleasure of work, has already commented that politicians are at their best after the age of sixty, because they understood far more about life at that time. What he calls 'impersonal interests' are vital, he says to happiness – and not just for politicians. We all need a refuge from our day-to-day worries if only because they help us solve those worries.

If we give all our energy, he says, to our family, work and money, we are unable to function well at any of them – because we never think about anything else. 'The man who can forget his work when it is over and not remember it until it begins again the next day is likely to do his work far better than the man who worries about it throughout the intervening hours.'

Why should this be? Our hinterland, he explains, has four functions. The first, and most important, is that it gives us a sense of proportion. When we are absorbed in our work 'we forget how small a part this is of the total of human activity'.

Second, it's consoling. We don't fall into the trap of overestimating our importance.

Third, it stops us constantly worrying at a problem. Obsession with work, for example, 'may make us work harder, but it will not make us work better,' Russell says.

Finally, it stops us from becoming fanatics: 'Which consists essentially in remembering one or two desirable things while forgetting all the rest.' Wilkinson desired to be the best goal kicker in rugby, and for a short time he was. When that was taken from him he could either obsess on what he had temporarily lost, or he could explore a world in which he would never win a World Cup, but which would still be there when excellence at rugby was denied to him – which will soon be the case for the rest of his life. Fanaticism may increase your focus but in the long run, Russell says, it won't increase your happiness.

HERE'S AN IDEA FOR YOU...

Film critic Mark Kermode balances reviewing films – 'an occupation which requires sitting silently in a darkened room' – with playing in skiffle band The Dodge Brothers. He's a 'cack-handed musician', but one who has deliberately chosen a hinterland that is as far from his day job as possible. If you can't escape from the work buzzing in your head, choose something entirely different.

48 STRATEGY AND TACTICS

The problem with power, Russell writes, is that we use too much attention trying to get things done, and not enough thinking about whether they're the right things to do.

Politicians without a sense of perspective, Russell complains, are too likely to risk everything for a short-term gain. 'The momentary battle on which you are engaged cannot be of such importance as to risk a backward step towards the darkness out of which we have been slowly emerging… you have, beyond your immediate activities, purposes that are distant and slowly unfolding.'

DEFINING IDEA…

Strategy is buying a bottle of fine wine when you take a lady out for dinner. Tactics is getting her to drink it.
~ FRANK MUIR

In his later years, Russell was to become one of the figureheads of the Campaign for Nuclear Disarmament, campaigning for countries to give up the bomb which in 1930 was not even a nightmare. His argument, that for little strategic gain it was ridiculous to imperil the entire planet and potentially obliterate human existence, was based on the same reasoning: if we are constantly chasing tactical advantages instead of paying attention to the greater need, we will not only fail to achieve happiness ourselves, but will destroy the chances of others to achieve happiness too. Even to the extent of ruining the chance of happiness of future generations, who aren't yet around to put their case.

How to solve the problem? For him, we needed to change the way we are educated. He advocated teaching history, but with the caveat that we should realise our potential future will be far longer than our recorded past – even if we, as individuals, will not be there for most of it. We should realise 'the minuteness of the planet on which we live', and that individuals can achieve greatness beyond the short-term priorities of the day, and that all of us have this possibility.

Would this help us to run our politics better? He thought so: 'A man who has once perceived, however temporarily and however briefly, what makes greatness of soul, can no longer be happy if he allows himself to be petty, self-seeking, troubled by trivial misfortunes, dreading what fate may have in store for him.'

'It is one of the defects of modern higher education that it has become too much a training in the acquisition of certain kinds of skill, and too little an enlargement of the mind and heart by an impartial survey of the world,' he laments. We value the short term over the long term, the action over the justification, presentation over reality and the tactical over the strategic. In his book *Obsessive Branding Disorder*, Lucas Conley points out that 77% of employees don't believe that their company's mission statement reflects the way they do business. When we talk about our strategy, it isn't meant to define what we decide to do until the next idea comes along. It is supposed to represent a permanent, integrated ideal.

Where do we start? With ourselves, Russell would say. By striving to live with honesty and a lack of self-importance we can live and teach by example, rather than trying to control others for short-term advantage.

HERE'S AN IDEA FOR YOU...

Corporate Social Responsibility is popular, but often prioritises image over long-term contribution. If your employer isn't doing enough, suggest something you think would be an improvement.

49 WHEN REALLY BAD STUFF HAPPENS

Coping with disagreements, disappointments and even bereavement can sometimes be easier if you have something else to do, Russell claims.

Thrice-married Bertrand Russell must have been a maddening person to have a row with. 'Few men except bachelors have never quarrelled with their wives,' he says. 'At such times, when in spite of the anxiety there is nothing to be done at the moment, one man will play chess, another will read detective stories, a third will become absorbed in popular astronomy, a fourth will console himself by reading about the excavations at Ur of the Chaldees.' This, in philosophy land, is how they roll.

DEFINING IDEA...

Grief drives men into habits of serious reflection, sharpens the understanding, and softens the heart.

~ JOHN ADAMS. SECOND PRESIDENT OF THE USA

For Russell, this is right and proper. These four are acting wisely, he says, because if you sit and worry about a problem when you can do nothing about it, you cannot solve the problem when you can do something about it. For example, when your partner has finished smashing crockery downstairs because you're in the spare room staring into a telescope again...

This line of reasoning, to our eyes, has several flaws – the most important being that you may not be required to solve a problem for your partner as much as to demonstrate selfless affection by giving your other half some loving attention. This might be a large part of the solution, especially if you have a habit of reading detective stories during moments of crisis.

On the other hand, there's a germ of truth in there. We all have the potential to respond to the emotion of a situation rather than its meaning, and sometimes that gets in the way of our ability to think constructively. Russell pushes this further, and applies it not just to arguments, but to bereavement.

'Grief is unavoidable and must be expected, but everything that can be done should be done to minimise it,' he says, adding that we should 'seek any distraction, however trivial, provided it is not in itself harmful and degrading.'

Instead of sitting in a closed house sobbing, you should sail your boat, drive your car, read a book on the philosophy of Bertrand Russell, anything but sentimentalise your grief. Unfortunately, if you don't have anything except work, money and family to interest you it's almost impossible to put bounds on your sorrow, or to put it into any meaningful proportion. The outpouring of grief for Princess Diana shows how powerful our need to project unexpressed grief and sorrow is if we cannot master those emotions.

Russell's diagnosis of feelings of bereavement: the sadness we feel combines self-pity and a futile wish for things to be different with the genuine feelings of loss. But beware. His prescription risks that in the search for happiness we don't just avoid sentimentality, but we avoid the natural process of grief altogether – which is denying our nature, not confronting it.

HERE'S AN IDEA FOR YOU...
What would you do if you lost your job, were separated from your family or suffered bereavement? Sooner or later, one of these things will happen, so making practical preparations and plans will allow you to grieve appropriately if the worst happens.

50 EFFORT, NOT RESIGNATION

We shouldn't just accept problems; we should strive to change them.

Happiness, Russell points out, does not 'drop into the mouth, like a ripe fruit'. If we sit at home and wait for someone to make us happy, we might wait a long time. If we all did this, we'd wait for ever. This is why *The Conquest of Happiness* got its title: happiness does not come unbidden.

Here's a quick experiment: to be in the top 10% of earners in the UK, would you have to earn £50,000, £100,000 or £200,000? The correct answer is £50,000. Most people guess the figure to be at least twice that.

The people we see in newspapers, on TV and in films have the sorts of lives that even people in the top 10% of wage earners could not afford. We are, overwhelmingly, not rich enough to 'live the dream'. We are mostly not talented enough to effortlessly earn respect. We are not, generally, considered beautiful except by one or two people. There's one chance in four that we won't reach the age of fifty.

'For all these reasons, happiness must be, for most men and women, an achievement rather than a gift of the gods,' Russell tells us.

Struggle does not guarantee success, but it makes it more likely. We desire success for ourselves and, as we saw earlier, work is a way in which we can achieve all types of success on our own terms. The struggle to find the right partner is another area where (though we do not acknowledge it) conspicuous success is rare. We accept the faults and failings of our partners with indulgence and amusement, and have a happy life as long as we are not stuck with someone we despise.

We also struggle to do the best we can for our children. It is a matter of great satisfaction when we teach them life skills, see their pride in achievement (which reflects well on us), nurse them better or squeeze them into the best school in the area by using whatever ruse we think we can get away with.

Finally, we need to struggle because for us, it's natural to try to exert power. We're accustomed to considering the desire for power a bad thing. In Russell's view, this is neither true nor realistic. 'Every kind of public work involves desire for some kind of power, unless it is undertaken solely with a view to wealth... the only man totally indifferent to power is the man totally indifferent to his fellow-men.'

We desire power to exercise it. That's neither good nor bad; the difference is whether we seek to exercise that power to increase the happiness in the world or to reduce it. We accept that, properly used, power is nothing but the ability to get good things done.

HERE'S AN IDEA FOR YOU...

Often we complain about our partners, our bosses or friends because they don't give us something we want: attention, more responsibility, engagement. Don't be passive. Tell them what you want, give them the choice to refuse you – and maybe change an unbearable situation.

51 RESIGNATION, NOT EFFORT

Yet effort alone cannot make you happy. Resignation helps you to become happier.

For some reason Southport, in Lancashire, has a vast war memorial right in the centre of the town. It's beautifully planned and constructed, and genuinely moving. It manages to make the point simultaneously that death is natural and affects us all, and that people who have died to help us deserve to be remembered with affection every day, not just once a year.

Carved on it is the inscription: 'Faithful to her we fell and rest content.' If I had been killed for no definable purpose by incompetent tactics in the war from hell between 1914 and 1918, I wouldn't be resting content. I'd be bloody angry.

DEFINING IDEA...

There are no failures, just experiences and your reactions to them.

~ TOM KRAUSE, MOTIVATIONAL SPEAKER

Southport's war memorial shows the usefulness and the limits of resignation in Russell's sense of the definition. On one hand, the elegance and dignity of the monument is a comfort for those who have been left alone or those who lost their friends. It's really built for them, not for the dead, who can't be content or angry any more. On the other hand, we shouldn't consider resignation to be helplessness; commemoration of wars is about settling with the past in order to look to the future.

We can't bring the victims of the First World War back, but remembering their sacrifice should give us pause when we clamour for war (if only it were more effective) and remind us that our freedoms are in part due to the sacrifices that others accepted as their duty. It also reminds us that individual lives are short and unpredictable.

Resignation has two outcomes, Russell says. One is despair, which is bad; the other is hope, which is good. Despair he equates closely with much religious feeling (though Christians, especially, would disagree in every way). By abandoning hope in this life and thinking about the next, a person 'will remain essentially useless and fundamentally unhappy'. It hardly needs saying that this doesn't account for the charity worker or the devout rich man who gives all his property to the poor.

The resignation of hope, Russell says, is part of accepting that we are but one small part of a larger world which, as long as we don't give up, can benefit from our actions. Our personal defeat can be part of a larger victory.

If you argue with your spouse, he tells us, regard your troubles in 'the way in which one regards a wet day'. Don't waste energy despairing when you miss a train or if your dinner is badly cooked. Don't obsess if your maid has not dusted properly (just as she, it seems, was wisely not obsessing over the consequences of dusting Bertrand Russell's study badly while he was writing his book).

Don't deny failure, don't just be 'content' with it, but accept it and try to put it right next time. 'Many active people are of opinion that the slightest grain of resignation, the faintest gleam of humour, would destroy the energy with which they do their work,' Russell concludes. 'These people are, in my opinion, mistaken.'

HERE'S AN IDEA FOR YOU...

To help you deal with failure don't imagine a perfect picture of you that is spoilt by it. Have a 'gallery' of realistic pictures, Russell says: clumsy you, say-the-wrong-thing you, mediocre-French you. Strive to be the best you can be, but don't worry that one slip will ruin everything.

52 THE STREAM OF LIFE

If we allow ourselves to contribute all we can to other living things, we can feel happy with what we have achieved.

The Conquest of Happiness asserts that we have far more influence over our happiness than we commonly believe; that our happiness does not depend on measurements like status, wealth or beauty, and that it is our primary responsibility to ensure our happiness and the happiness of others.

DEFINING IDEA...

The best way to cheer yourself up is to try to cheer somebody else up.
– MARK TWAIN

We do this, Russell concludes, by accepting that we are part of 'the stream of life'. 'Such a man feels himself a citizen of the universe, enjoying freely the spectacle that it offers and the joys that it affords, untroubled by the thought of death because he feels himself not really separate from those who will come after him,' he says in his closing chapter.

We need to respect our own needs and be aware of them when we act. As Russell points out, if someone says that he wants to make you happy, but that he's going to give up the prospect of happiness as a result, it's hard to respect his actions.

We need to accept the inevitability of death. Russell did, even though it was a long time coming – he was ninety-seven when he died.

We need to fight our tendency to self-importance. He believed that it is our responsibility not to make the existence of others less happy if at all possible.

Most of all, we should be open to ideas that can make us happy, whether or not others approve.

Russell was trying to cure a modern epidemic: unhappiness. UK government figures show that in any year, twelve per cent of people experience depression. Our society has provided a range of pills to alter the mood of those who are diagnosed as suffering from depression. We are a medicated, unhappy society, and the access to money, entertainment, distraction and stimulation which we have today does not seem to be the answer.

We might disagree with some of what Russell has to say, but we should admire him for reminding us that if we are not happy, we are missing the most important aspect of being alive. Striving for happiness is our responsibility. It requires strength, but an uncommon strength to be open, giving and flexible – not, in Russell's words, 'a hard separate entity like a billiard-ball that can have no relation with other such entities except that of collision'.

It's time to stop colliding and join Russell's stream of life where, he knew, 'the greatest joy is to be found'.

HERE'S AN IDEA FOR YOU...

Be a hedonist: do one thing today which is for your pleasure only. The only rule is that it does not directly harm someone else. Do another tomorrow. And one the day after that. It's time to claim back happiness, one moment at a time.

INDEX

Lightning Source UK Ltd.
Milton Keynes UK
09 April 2010
152553UK00001B/7/A